Lancaster bomber

S0-BYG-634

DB Tubbs had his first flight in a
Le Rhone-engined Avro 504K
as a small boy and has been
interested in flying ever since.
He has contributed articles on
air fighting to Purnell's History
of the First World War, and has
written a number of books about
Vintage cars and motor racing.

Lancaster bomber

D B Tubbs

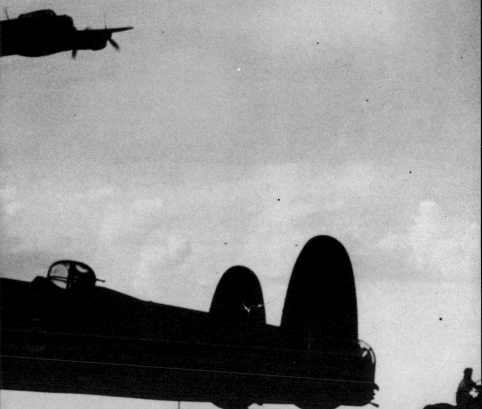

BB

Editor-in-Chief: Barrie Pitt
Editor: David Mason
Art Director: Sarah Kingham
Picture Editor: Robert Hunt
Consultant Art Editor: Dennis Piper
Designer: Michael Frost
Illustration: David Penney
Photographic Research: Jonathan Moore
Cartographer: David Penney

Contents

The perfect 'heavy'?

Introduction by Group Captain Leonard Cheshire, VC, DSO, DFC

The Lancaster was by far the most effective heavy bomber which the Royal Air Force despatched on war operations. Much more robust and reliable than its predecessors, the Wellington and the Whitley, it could also carry a heavier load and fly farther than its contemporaries, the Stirling and the Halifax. It was the eventual product of the prewar specification which mercifully foresaw what was coming and which, in the view of many, turned the tide that otherwise would have engulfed us.

The Luftwaffe was designed primarily as a support arm to the Wehrmacht, not as a force capable of operating independently and in its own right. All-conquering as it was in Europe and, one might add, totally ruthless, it was relatively impotent once the advance of the German army was halted by the English Channel, and was outfought by a fighter force numerically far inferior. The RAF, on the other hand, had always regarded itself as an attacking and offensive force in its own right and if necessary, independent of the other services. But for the wisdom of those who in the mid-1930s foresaw the need for a heavy bomber capability history might have

been very different. Out of the specification that was then laid ᵤown came first the Stirling and then the Halifax and Manchester. The Manchester was a failure, but from it was developed the Lancaster which came into operational service in March 1942 and thereafter became the mainstay of Bomber Command. By April 1944 Bomber Command had an available striking force of just over 1,000 aircraft, out of which 614 were Lancasters. A year later, in the last month of the war, the striking force had risen to more than 1,600 aircraft of which 1,088 were Lancasters.

To those who, like myself, graduated from other types of Heavies, the Lancaster was a totally new experience. To say that it was the perfect Heavy is clearly an exaggeration, for such could really never exist, yet that is more or less what many called it. It had the strength to survive damage that would have toppled other aircraft out of the sky; the gentleness and margin for error that infused confidence in its crew and the manoeuvrability to make possible the brilliant feat of Gibson and those who flew with him on that remarkable mission in May 1943 against the

Moehne and Eder dams. As was later demonstrated, it could be flown safely and efficiently at extreme low level for the purpose of target marking by night; and when Barnes Wallis produced his deep penetration bombs, first the relatively small Tallboy and then the 10-ton Grand Slam, it provided a platform from which a Squadron bombing average error of something like forty yards was achieved from a height of 16,000 feet. It was one of the few aircraft ever to have proved itself capable of a great deal more than had been envisaged in its original design, and an analysis of the figures show that it contributed more to the destruction of military and industrial targets in Hitler's Germany than any other type of aircraft, whether British or American.

This book might appear aimed exclusively at the professional or the specialist, for it contains an astonishing wealth of fact and detail so that one can hardly envisage a technical or historical question being asked about the aircraft to which the answer is not to be found. Yet a broader and more human canvas is also covered, and one feels that whoever might choose to read these pages could not fail to find something to interest and attract. For five long and most wearisome years, almost daily, Bomber Command carried the war into Germany. Some will argue that it had no right to do this, others that it was ineffective, others again that its priorities were wrong. Be this as it may, and granting that mistakes unquestionably were made, the fact remains that Bomber Command did carry the war at a time when there was no other possible way of doing so, and pinned down perhaps as much as a fifth of the vital elements in Hitler's armaments that otherwise would have been free to engage the armies on the battlefield. Those who never knew those days will find here the essential facts about the conditions under which the Lancaster operated, the life of the crews who flew them, and indeed

the unfolding of the whole campaign in the air over the Nazi fortress of Europe. For those who lived through, and experienced, them, familiar sights and sounds and turns of phrase will find their way back into the mind. One can almost feel oneself picking one's steps forward along the fuselage to the cockpit, settling into the seat and then finally starting up the engines, with their familiar reassuring look and sound. Such a memory is valid so long as it is not an end in itself, but a means of remembering the sacrifice with which peace was bought and the duty that each has to struggle as best one may to make that peace a lasting reality, not just a far-away dream.

Today, when aircraft come out of a common pool and are flown first by one crew and then by another, one perhaps half forgets the personal relationship that then existed between a man and his machine, and how much this relationship meant. To most pilots the aircraft ceased to be just a machine and became almost another person, at least an ally, a being to be cherished and looked after, who in turn would respond to one's own demands in time of extreme emergency, perhaps to an almost superhuman degree. We each owned our own aircraft, and almost more important still our own ground crew, both of whom we looked upon as part of ourselves and which only under dire necessity would we lend to anyone else. Proportionately as these ties of mutual understanding and confidence developed, one flew to greater effect, was the more likely to survive damage or injury and served out one's time in the squadron with more peace of mind. It is, I think, a sense of the debt that we as air crew owed to all those, both great and humble, who played a part either in the design, or the construction, or the maintenance of the aircraft and its equipment, upon which so much depended, that these excellent pages leave with me – a debt that in all walks of life one so easily forgets.

The vultures disperse

**Britain's last heavy bomber of the
Second World War, the Avro Lancaster**

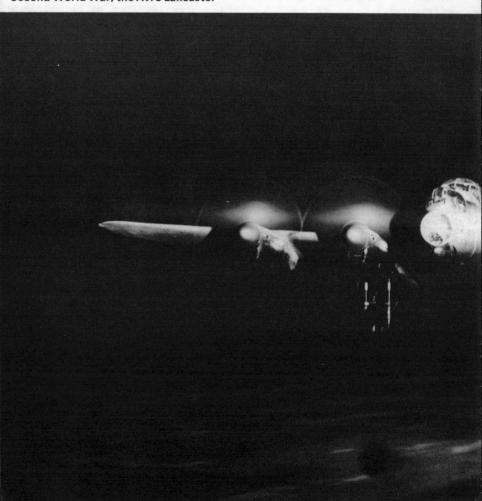

The Avro 683 Lancaster was the last of the RAF's four-engined bombers to enter war service, and the best. Air Chief Marshal Sir Arthur Harris, Commander in Chief, Bomber Command, called it the greatest single factor in winning the Second World War. Hyperbole, perhaps, but the big Avro bred hyperbole as lesser designs breed criticism. 'Its efficiency was incredible', wrote Harris in 1947, 'both in performance and in the way in which it could be saddled with ever increasing loads without breaking the camel's back. It is astonishing that so small an aircraft as the Lancaster could so easily take the enormous Grand Slam bomb, a weapon which no other aircraft could, or yet can, carry. The Lancaster far surpassed all other types of heavy bombers. Not only were there fewer accidents with this than with other types; throughout the war the casualty rate of Lancasters was consistently below that of other types.'

An ex-Mosquito pilot recently put it another way: 'The Lanc was fantastically strong. If there was one-quarter of one left by the German defences, that quarter would fly home.' Then he added: 'Not bad, really, for a lash-up!'

'Lash-up' the Lancaster certainly was not. It was an inspired improvisation. When the Avro 679 twin-engined Manchester failed, let down by its over-worked and under-developed Rolls-Royce Vulture engines, the airframe was hurriedly redesigned to take four of the well-tried Merlins, as

Above: The Avro Manchester, forerunner of the Lancaster. *Below:* The twin Vulture-engined Manchester offered neither great range nor heavy bomb-carrying capacity. *Bottom:* The Handley-Page Hampden suffered from the same power-weight restrictions as the Manchester

used in Spitfire and Hurricane. 'Once the Vultures had dispersed', as one pilot wryly put it, the big bomber went ahead fast. The Merlin became quite the most successful of all Rolls-Royce engines named after birds of prey. The coincidence that the new engines were Merlins and that Merlin was also the name of King Arthur's resident necromancer, possibly accounts for the Lancaster proving to be, in the slang of its day, a 'wizard' aircraft.

The speed with which Lancasters entered service was also something of a record. The first prototype made its maiden flight on 8th January 1941, a second was flying on 13th May and the first production aircraft, taking shape on the Manchesters' assembly line, took off on 31st October from the Woodford factory of A V Roe and Co Ltd for the RAF experimental aerodrome at Boscombe Down. During September 44 (Rhodesian) Squadron, commanded by Wing Commander R A B Learoyd, VC, had watched a demonstration of the prototype, BT308, and learned with glee that Lancasters were to replace their old Handley-Page Hampdens (two 1,000hp Bristol Pegasus radials), for undeniably the 'Flying Panhandle' was past its best work. The squadron received its first two Lancasters as a most welcome gift on Christmas Eve 1941. The type had progressed from maiden flight to squadron service in less than twelve months.

Historically there was some excuse for the Manchester's two engines. When German rearmament forced the RAF to plan heavy bombers in 1936 the only four-engined type the service had ever possessed was the Handley-Page V1500, constructed in small numbers for bombing Berlin from bases in England right at the end of the First World War. The 'super-Handley' arrived too late to be operational and was too expensive for peacetime development. Postwar economics did not favour four-engined aeroplanes and there were many in the Service who

Above: Air Chief Marshal Sir Arthur 'Bomber' Harris.
Below: Merlin-engined Spitfires with Lancasters behind

agreed with C G Grey, Editor of *The Aeroplane*, who used to say that four-engined machines must be less reliable than single-engined because the risk of engine failure was four times as great! Be that as it may, the Service was to go without four-engined machines until the rearmament activity of the late 1930s, during half of which period the principal heavy bombers were the Atlantic-conquering Vickers Vimy (two 360hp Rolls-Royce Eagle VIIIs) and its derivative the Vickers Virginia (various marks of Napier Lion), whose resemblance to a grand piano was so marked as to be unmentionable. Troop-carrier versions of the Vimy and Virginia (Vernon and Victoria) were also developed, having an eleven-seater

cabin fuselage shaped like an Easter egg. It was while commanding a Vernon squadron in Iraq that a certain Wing Commander A T Harris in 1924 made clear where his future interests would lie. 'By sawing a sighting hole in the nose of our troop carriers', he wrote in *Bomber Offensive*, 'and making our own bomb-racks we converted them into what were really the first of of the postwar long-range heavy bombers'.

In 1932 the Service overcame its ancient mistrust of monoplanes, ordering Barnes Wallis's Vickers Wellington and the Handley-Page Hampden. Both these machines were twin engined, and so was the Armstrong Whitworth Whitley of 1934. Not until 1936 was there a call for four-

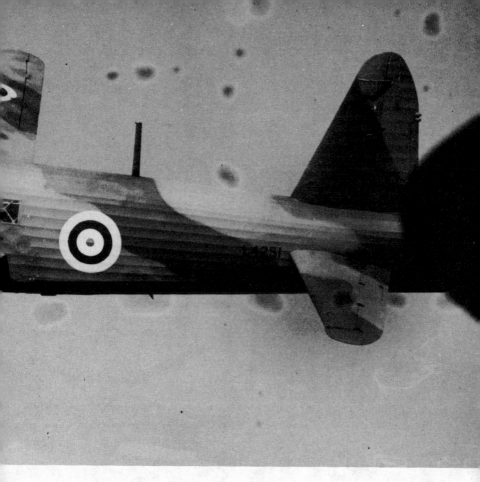

The twin-engined Vickers Wellington. It was from the same drawing board as the Dambusters bomb

engined machines, and even then, one of the two specifications issued for all-metal monoplane heavy bombers called for two engines only. Old habits die hard.

One of the requirements of Air Ministry specification P.13/36 was that the all-metal mid-wing monoplanes concerned should carry a bomb load of 12,000 lb, a formidable load for two engines in the year 1936, and one which caused some consternation. Faced with a similar problem in 1918, Handley-Page had doubled-up the engines in each nacelle of the V/1500, using one tractor and one pusher, thus securing four-engined performance with little more than twin-engined drag. Now attempts were made to do roughly the same thing in more

sophisticated fashion. The specification called for the use of Rolls-Royce Vulture engines, rated rather optimistically at 1,760hp, one of the most powerful units then in production. To obtain this output Rolls-Royce engineers took many components of the existing Peregrine Vee twelve, so that the engine looked like a normal Vee twelve with an inverted Vee twelve below it. The four banks of six Peregrine cylinders therefore were arranged to form a twenty-four cylinder X, at the heart of which was a single seven-bearing twelve-throw crankshaft. On each crankpin ran two H-

13

Avro's 504 biplane, First World War hero
of the raid on Friedrichshafen

section nickel steel forged connecting-rods, one plain and one forked, the latter having a nickel steel bearing block lined inside and out with lead bronze – as in the Merlin. Even with twin radiators slung below, the Vulture engine was neat, and great power was produced for little drag; but cynics who forecast maintenance problems, lubrication troubles and bearing failure for this complicated engine were right.

In the Manchester airframe designed for these engines the Avro company had a winner—strong, clean and, after teething troubles, safe and controllable. The firm had a splendid history going back to pioneer days when their founder Alliott Verdon Roe had been warned off Lea Marshes and

Roy Chadwick, designer of the Avro 504 and, later, the Lancaster

Brooklands motor racing track as a nuisance. Within a few years Roe was an established manufacturer, and his 504 biplane had earned fame first by a daring (and successful) RNAS raid on the Zeppelin sheds at Friedrichshafen and second as the standard RAF trainer from mid-war days until the nineteen-thirties. The 504 was designed by one Roy Chadwick, and the Manchester/Lancaster was also his work. In charge of production was another Roy: a tough, forthright man named Dobson, who had joined as a draughtsman and then set to work in the hangars. In 1915 or so he had saved a test pilot's life, and his own, by crawling forward along the shiny turtle-decked top of a bomber fuselage to adjust the tail-heavy trim of an experimental machine. Later he became managing director of A V Roe and Co Ltd and was knighted. Sir Roy

Dobson was one of the most formidable figures in the British aircraft industry.

Although evidently under-powered the Manchester went into production, 200 being ordered, of which the first entered service with 207 Squadron in November 1940. A spate of modifications followed; perhaps the situation is best summed up by a conversation reported by the late Wing Commander Guy Gibson VC, DSO, DFC, in his book 'Enemy Coast Ahead'.

Gibson was introduced to the Manchester by his friend Flight Lieutenant Dunlop Mackenzie as he took command of 106 Squadron. 'These Manchesters', said Mackenzie, 'they're awful. The actual kite's all right, but it's the engines. They're fine when they keep turning, but they don't often do so. We have had an awful lot of prangs . . . If you're hit in one engine you've had it.'

Gibson raised an eyebrow. 'But surely they will fly on one engine?' 'Some will, some won't. A fellow called "Kipper" Herring from 61 Squadron brought one back all the way from Berlin on one engine, and got the DSO for it, but he's an exception.'

A few days later P J Dunlop Mackenzie was killed; Guy Gibson went on flying Manchesters and became, of course, one of the outstanding Lancaster pilots of the war, whose 'dambusting' sortie with 617 Squadron is treated later.

In mid-1940 it was decided to scrap the twin Vultures and redesign the airframe to accept four of the well-tried Merlin X engines of 1,145hp each.

Sir Roy Dobson, production manager and later managing director of A V Roe

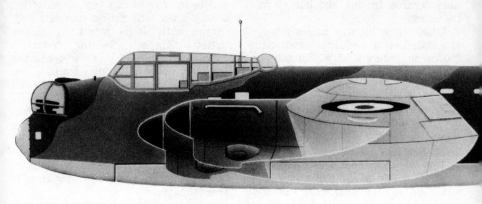

The Avro Type 683 Lancaster Prototype (BT308) was developed from the two-engined Avro Manchester, whose Rolls-Royce Vulture engines had been a failure. The fuselage was a standard Manchester one, as were the triple vertical tail surfaces, married to a wing with a new centre section to accommodate the four Rolls-Royce Merlins. The type flew for the first time on 9th January, 1941 and was an immediate success. The triple vertical surfaces were soon replaced by larger double surfaces at the ends of the horizontal tailplane. The finish was standard Bomber Command green and earth upper surfaces with yellow undersurfaces. The

Hurricanes escort a Stirling in its bombing role

first designation of the type was Manchester III, but this was soon changed to Lancaster. BT308 was handed over to No 44 Squadron at Waddington in September 1941 for squadron evaluation and crew training. *Engines:* Four Rolls-Royce Merlin X, 1,145hp each. *Speed:* 275mph at 15,000 feet. Climb: 250 feet per minute. Ceiling: 19,000 feet. *Range:* 2,000 miles. *Armament:* Six .303-inch Browning machine guns and up to 18,000lbs of bombs. *Weight empty/loaded:* 36,500lbs/62,500lbs. *Span:* 100 feet. *Length:* 69 feet 6 inches

Manchesters actually on the production line were altered to take a brace of Merlins (1,280hp Merlin XXs after the first prototype) in the centre section, while the mid-section of the wings was redesigned to accept an extra Merlin each side, slightly set back. Wing ribs were spaced out to increase the span from the Manchester's 90 feet 1 inch to a round 100 feet, later increased to 102 feet exactly. Coyly, the new four-engined machine was known at first as the Manchester III, and even introduced to the squadrons as a 'Manchester variant'. Renamed Lancaster, the new version quickly lived down its twin-engined past, to emerge as an aeroplane in its own right, and oddly enough as one of those designs universally accepted as 'thoroughbred'. Vultures, so often the end of a chapter, had in this case provided a beginning.

Of all the machines built to the 1936 bomber specifications the Lancaster proved far the most successful.

Wisely, in view of what happened to the Manchester, the Handley-Page company, who had submitted tenders for a twin-engined machine, redesigned it at an early stage to accept four Bristol engines. This became the Handley-Page Halifax. Two tenders were received for A M Specification B.12/36, the four-engined class. One of these, designed for Supermarine by R J Mitchell, of Spitfire fame, was destroyed by bombing in 1940 and not proceeded with. The other was the Short Sterling, the first four-engined bomber to enter war service with the RAF. Rather 'Vintage' in its handling, the Sterling appealed particularly to the older generation of pilots – what one of them termed the 'pre-syncromesh school'; it was more difficult to fly than the Lancaster, and less forgiving. Stirlings gave excellent service both as bombers and glider tugs, although their lack of speed and ceiling made them much more vulnerable than the Halifax and Lancaster.

Construction
and survival

The Avro Lancaster Mk I

Two members of a squadron were discussing the source of a Lancaster's strength. One, from the motor industry, talked of 'integral body-cum-chassis construction'. The other, an RAF chaplain, murmured that the strength lay in the nave and transept, adding with tongue in cheek that pilots sat in the choir. They were both right. The central portion was immensely strong – doubly so. Reinforced in the fore-and-aft direction by a flat floor which formed also the roof of the bomb bay, to which bombs of up to ten tons' weight were slung, it was crossed by the two waist-high main spars extending sideways from the fuselage and carrying a Merlin on its triangulated steel-tube mounting at each end. Specially strong wing ribs

absorbed the loadings behind each engine, and into this key structure formed by front spar and engine mountings were fed loads from the Dowty oleo-pneumatic undercarriage. When retracted the undercarriage legs were housed in rearward extensions of the inboard engine nacelles. To this immensely sturdy cruciform structure the mainplanes and rear section of the fuselage were bolted..

Guy Gibson, introducing the Lancaster in 'Enemy Coast Ahead', speaks cryptically of 'factories who turned out the new aircraft in conditions peculiar only to this country'. The British aircraft industry, like British motor manufacturers, has never shied away from decentralisation. The Lancaster was designed as a series of sub-

assemblies capable of being built in any convenient factory, ready for dispatch to one or more central assembly plants with aerodromes alongside. When production outgrew the resources of the Avro company, with main works at Chadderton and final assembly at Woodford, the Lancaster Aircraft Group was formed comprising the parent company based on Manchester and Yeadon, together with Armstrong Whitworth Aircraft (Baginton), Metropolitan Vickers (Moseley Road, Manchester), Vickers-Armstrong (Castle Bromwich), Vickers-Armstrong (Chester), and the Austin Motor Company (Longbridge, Birmingham). Lancasters were built also in Canada by Victory Aircraft. Engines for Mark I and Mark VII aircraft came from Rolls-Royce plants in Britain, and for Mark III from the Packard Motor Co, Detroit. Mark II Lancasters were fitted with air-cooled Bristol Hercules engines, and the

Canadian-built Mark X used Packard-built Merlins. So there was considerable coming and going of Lancaster parts between factories, docks and aerodromes.

The Lancaster, in the manufacturer's own words, was 'a four-engined mid-wing heavy bomber of all-metal construction', weighing 16½ tons in standard form and 29 tons laden. 'Specials' weighed just under 16 tons unladen and 32 tons with full load. The fuselage was of elliptical section, tapering only slightly throughout its length: wide enough at cabin level for a pilot and flight engineer to sit side by side, it still gave room at the extreme tail for a heavily clad 'tail end Charlie' to swing round in his hydraulically-operated gun turret. The wing was tapered in plan with rounded wing tips and dihedral angle only on the sections outboard of the inner engines. The tailplane carried a vertical fin and rudder at each end,

shaped rather like a Zulu shield
upside down. The four Merlins were
housed in streamlined nacelles, each
with its radiator below, in front of the
leading edge of the wings, and they
drove three-bladed variable-pitch constant-speed airscrews.

So much can be learned from photographs. Less obvious is the fact that
wings and fuselage were made up from
a number of sub-assemblies which
could be made in different factories.
The fuselage, for example, was made
as five portions; firstly: nose, complete with gun turret; secondly:
cabin, with stations for pilot, flight
engineer, navigator and wireless operator; thirdly: centre section proper,
separated from the cabin by armoured
doors – just long enough for a rest bed,
being bounded fore and aft by the wing
spars; it extended side ways to include
the inboard engine mountings;
fourthly: fuselage, containing mid-
upper and, when fitted, lower gun

A 'Queen Mary' trailer used to transport
the Lancaster fuselage to its assembly
point

turrets; fifthly; rear fuselage with tail
gun turret. For transport the fuselage
was handled in three sections: nose,
with cabin; centre section; sections 4
and 5 combined. Vast slabs of dark-
green camouflage on sixty-foot 'Queen
Mary' trailers were a frequent sight
on wartime roads. An advantage of the
sub-assembly system was that whole
sections could be replaced when
damaged from components held in
store. Sometimes, even, an undam-
aged section from an aircraft otherwise 'written off' was returned to one
of the factories to take its place on
the assembly line of new aircraft.

The fuselage was a stressed-skin
monocoque hull designed to be as
simple and straightforward as possible. The structure was almost
entirely of light alloy, an Alclad skin

23

(Duralumin coated on both sides with pure aluminium to resist corrosion) being riveted to the outer flanges of channel-section formers pressed from the same material and further supported by longitudinal stringers notched into the formers and running the entire length of the fuselage. The stringers were attached to the formers by angle-brackets riveted to both, and similar but larger brackets attached the formers to the floor. Formers for the front end rear sections were elliptical; those amidships, where the Lancaster stowed its bombs, were D-shaped, the flat side doubling as cabin floor and roof to the bomb bay, from

Mk II Lancaster powered by Bristol Hercules air-cooled radial engines

which the bombs were hung on slips. The overall elliptical shape hereabouts was completed by the bomb-doors, hinged at the sides and opening downwards. By the use of D-shaped formers Roy Chadwick provided an unimpeded bomb-bay, an improvement upon that of the Stirling, for example, which was spoilt by a cross-member. Lancasters Marks I and III could carry 4,000-lb bombs. Mark II (Hercules) aircraft and the Mark X from Canada were fitted with longer bomb doors, enabling them to take the 8,000-lb. On Mark I/III Special aircraft carrying dam-buster, Tallboy or Grand Slam, bomb doors were dispensed with altogether.

At the junctions between main sub-assemblies, known for obvious reasons

as 'transport joints' the formers were of different and heavier section. Adjacent sections were joined by special high-tensile bolts, and as all parts were accurately jig-built there was complete inter-changeability. Wings were built and attached in the same way. Lancaster main planes were constructed in seventeen parts, these being normally assembled into larger structures before despatch. The wing could be handled for transport in three, five or seven portions.

The core or hub of the aircraft, the Padre's 'transept', was doubly strong being formed by the intersection of the bomb-bay/cabin floor and the two spars of the wing. Each spar was built up from a top and a bottom boom, these being light-alloy (L.40 or DTD

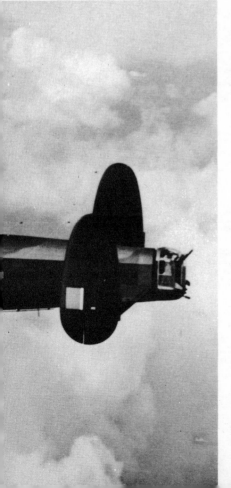

364) extrusions, milled out to a channel section except at certain points where metal was left for greater strength. These booms were united by an Alclad plate forming a web stiffened at intervals by vertical channels and by L-section stiffeners riveted on. The webs formed the front face of the front spar and the rear face of the rear spar; the spars were supported by ribs built up from Alclad pressings, and attached to the vertical stiffening members on the spar webs. The wings were constructed in the same way, from spars and ribs, with Alclad covering riveted in place except where panels were needed for access to the fuel tanks, where Simmonds self-locking nuts were used. There were six self-sealing tanks: two of 580 gallons, between the fuselage and inboard engines, two of 383 gallons placed midway between inboard and outboard engines, and two holding 114 gallons between the outboard engines and wingtips, a total capacity of 2,154 gallons. A fuel-up took about twenty minutes. Normally engines drew from tanks on their own side, but elaborate cross-feed arrangements were made in case tanks were damaged. These were looked after by the flight engineer.

How, it may be wondered, were the mainplanes attached to the centre section? This is well described in the manufacturer's own words: 'The outboard end of the [centre section] booms are further strengthened by steel plates fitted on their front and rear faces and secured to them by a number of bolts. These steel plates and the booms which they enclose are drilled at their outboard ends for one large bolt in each boom, which forms the main anchorage for the mainplane root to the centre section. The wing root which is similarly strengthened is attached to the centre section by forged steel shackles, one on the front and one on the rear of each boom, the whole being secured together by two high-tensile steel bolts which must be a good close fit in their holes. In addition, a fishplate is bolted to the

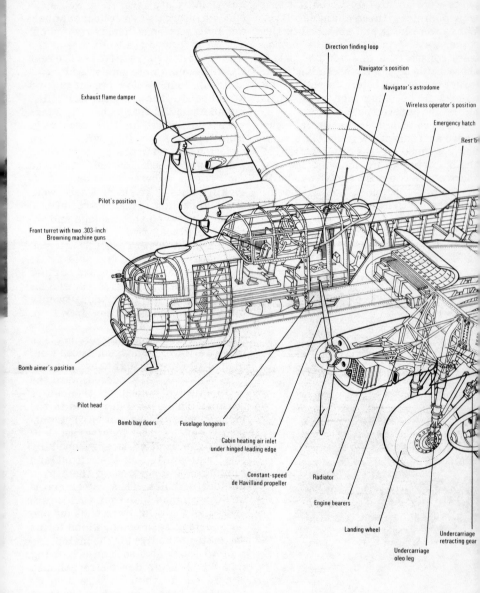

Direction finding loop

Navigator's position

Navigator's astrodome

Wireless operator's position

Emergency hatch

Rest b⌐

Exhaust flame damper

Pilot's position

Front turret with two .303-inch
Browning machine guns

Bomb aimer's position

Pilot head

Bomb bay doors

Fuselage longeron

Cabin heating air inlet
under hinged leading edge

Constant-speed
de Havilland propeller

Radiator

Engine bearers

Landing wheel

Undercarriage
retracting gear

Undercarriage
oleo leg

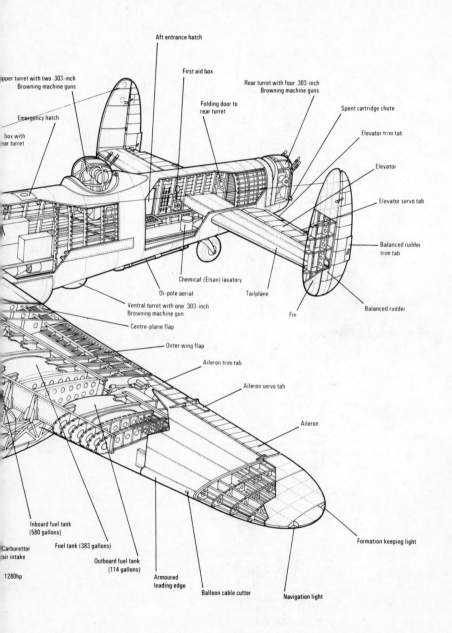

Aft entrance hatch

First aid box

Upper turret with two .303-inch
Browning machine guns

Rear turret with four .303-inch
Browning machine guns

Emergency hatch

Folding door to
rear turret

Spent cartridge chute

box with
ear turret

Elevator trim tab

Elevator

Elevator servo tab

Balanced rudder
trim tab

Chemical (Elsan) lavatory

Di-pole aerial

Tailplane

Balanced rudder

Ventral turret with one .303-inch
Browning machine gun

Fin

Centre-plane flap

Outer wing flap

Aileron trim tab

Aileron servo tab

Aileron

Formation keeping light

Inboard fuel tank
(580 gallons)

Carburettor
air intake

Fuel tank (383 gallons)

Outboard fuel tank
(114 gallons)

1280hp

Armoured
leading edge

Balloon cable cutter

Navigation light

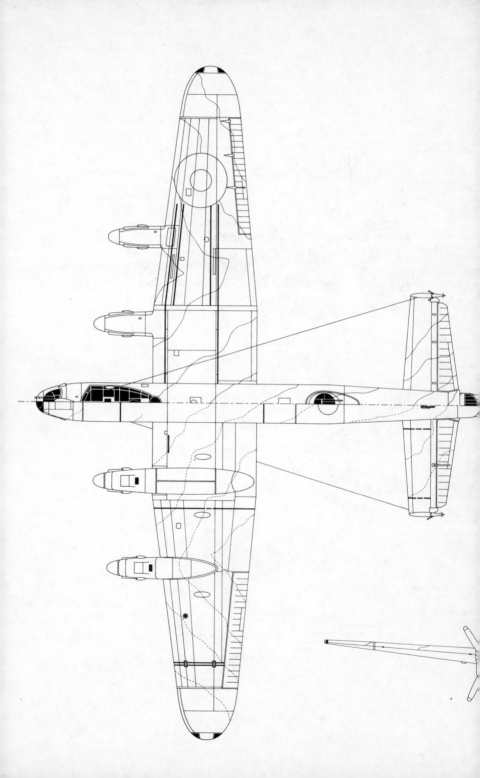

The Avro Lancaster Type 683 Lancaster Mk I (B I from 1942), the first true production Lancaster, flew in October 1941 in the form of L7527. The B I continued in service until the end of the war, and even after its end in the case of a few special modifications. The Lancaster was structurally immensely strong and capable of absorbing considerable combat damage.

Engines: Four R-R Merlin XX, 1,280hp each (later models had Merlin 22 or 24s). *Crew:* 7. *Speed:* 275mph at 15,000 feet fully loaded. *Climb:* 250 feet per minute. *Ceiling:* 19,000 feet. *Range:* 2,530 miles with 7,000lbs load, 1,730 miles with 12,000lbs load and 1,550 miles with 22,000lbs load. *Armament:* Frazer-Nash 5 nose turret with two .303-inch machine guns, Frazer-Nash 50 mid-upper turret with two .303-inch Browning machine guns, Frazer-Nash 20 tail turret with four .303-inch Browning machine guns, and Frazer-Nash 64 ventral turret with one .303-inch Browning machine gun (the last dispensed with in Lancaster Is of Nos 1 and 5 Groups in 1944). Some late production models had a Frazer-Nash 121 tail turret with four .303-inch Browning Mk II machine guns or a Frazer-Nash 82 tail turret with two .5-inch Browning machine guns. Bomb load on all standard Lancaster Is was up to 18,000lbs. *Weight empty/loaded:* 37,000/65,000lbs. *Span:* 102 feet. *Length:* 69 feet 6 inches

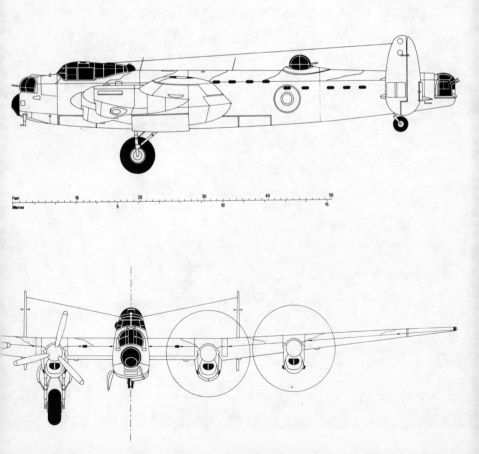

webs of the centre section and wing spars to take the shear load.'

Centre section ribs were of two types: four extra strong ones built up from channel-section extrusions carried the main loads in the bays immediately behind the inboard engines;

Left-hand drive cockpit of a Lancaster from the flight engineer's seat

inboard of them came special box-form ribs fabricated from Alclad sheet to carry the inboard fuel tanks. The tanks were inserted from below and held in place by steel straps. Each inboard tank, full, weighed close on two tons. In the centre-section trailing edge were housed the inboard sections of the landing-flaps, hydraulically operated, like the mainplane

flaps adjoining them, from a cylinder within the fuselage, and inter-connected by means of a universally-jointed control rod.

Each of the Merlins was carried on a tubular steel mounting bolted to two steel brackets on the main spar and one on the rear spar, providing three-point attachment. The entire leading edge of the centre section on each side

was hinged to give access to the controls, cabin heaters and other gear mounted on the front face of the main spar. Accidents were not uncommon at first through these being left undone. The leading edges of the main-planes were built up from ribs and stringers, strongly reinforced and provided with balloon-cable cutters. The wing-tips, built up in the same way as the wings, were detachable, and bolted to the outboard end of the main spar. They carried navigation and station-keeping lights in moulded Perspex fairings. The trailing edges of the mass-balanced ailerons were fabric covered.

The tail assembly of a Lancaster was an impressive structure, three feet wider in span than a Tiger Moth's main planes; the two halves of the tail plane met at the centre line of the fuselage, to which they were attached by four big bolts. At each end rose a vertical fin carried on a fin-post bolted to the end of the tail plane spars. Fins and rudder spars were constructed from duralumin pressings reinforced with steel angles, unlike the tail plane which was built on mainplane lines. The leading edge of the fin was reinforced and stiffened with laminated mahogany – like an old-fashioned propeller – before the metal skin was attached by counter-sunk wood-screws. Fin and rudder were both metal covered; the ele-vators, fabricated from welded steel tubing, were fabric covered. Inside the horn of the rudder were mass-balance weights, and external bronze balance weights of streamline form were carried on projecting prongs. Trim-mers on the rudder, elevators and ailerons could be set as necessary by handwheels beside the pilot's seat and, to lighten the control movements, servo tabs were fitted to elevators and ailerons. Also present was 'George', whose official name was Automatic Pilot Mark IV.

As befitted a four-engined aircraft the Lancaster had a bewildering array of dials and levers and buttons, many of them controlling auxiliary services run by electricity, hydraulic power, compressed air and vacuum systems. Sometimes several systems might be used to work a single component, and there were of course purely mechanical arrangements – rather, one suspects, to the pilots' relief. For example the rudder and elevator controls comprised simple light—alloy push-pull tubes running the length of the fuselage, supported in Tufnol bearings housed in the arched formers which gave the fuselage its shape. Ailerons were similarly controlled, with the addition of the chains, sprockets and bell-cranks necessary to turn rotary motion of the pilot's control wheel into up-and-down motion at the ailerons. Aileron, elevator and rudder trimmers were worked via handwheels on a pedestal beside the pilot's seat and operated by cables running over Vickers pulleys. The throttle controls, too, were mechanical, operating by a system of chains, sprockets and tie-rods for each engine; a simple cam-and-lever device was arranged to sound an electric buzzer in the event of the engines being completely throttled back (as for landing) without the undercarriage being locked in the 'down' position.

Power for raising and lowering the undercarriage came from the hydraulic system, kept up to pressure by a Dowty pump driven by each of the inboard engines supplying a hydraulic accumulator mounted aft of the reservoir in the fuselage. The hydraulics also operated bomb doors, landing flaps, hot/cold air intakes for the engines and movement of the gun turrets. They also worked a small rotary control valve for the fuel-jettison system. An emergency hand pump was supplied in case the hydraulic lines should be shot away or both inboard engines stopped for any reason. 'Operation by means of the hand pump is not difficult', the manufacturers stated wryly, 'but is somewhat slow'. Aircrew experienced in

lowering flaps and undercarriage by hand have endorsed this judgment. All told, the system, including nose, tail and mid-upper turrets, contained some thirty gallons of hydraulic fluid. It had plenty to do. A second emergency system for flaps and undercarriage was worked by compressed air.

Compressed air was used also for the brakes, supplied from a bottle charged by a compressor on a starboard engine. A lever on the pilot's control wheel applied the brakes for landing or parking, and the machine was steered on the ground by kicking the rudder-bar, thus braking one wheel at a time. Compressed air was also used for the electro-mechanical rams which opened and closed the radiator shutters, thus keeping the engines at the right temperature, and to operate the supercharger controls. It also activated the servo controls of the automatic pilot.

As the fuel tanks were emptied by their pumps, nitrogen was fed in under pressure to reduce the fire risk, for unlike the Luftwaffe the RAF put all its faith in petrol, never diesel fuel.

There were other systems to be tended by the ground crews. Oxygen pipes led from fifteen storage cylinders (in five rows of three in a crate under the rest bed) to each crew station. Certain flying and navigation instruments were worked by vacuum power. This was maintained by two Pesco pumps, one on each inboard engine. Sometimes the systems were mixed. To feather an airscrew or change its pitch – the equivalent of free-wheeling or changing gear in a car – the flight engineer pressed a button on the instrument panel. This closed an electrical relay circuit, which energised a solenoid, which in turn switched on an electric motor for operating the auxiliary oil-pump, and this pump built up pressure of 300-400 lbs per square inch, enough to move the actuating cams and turn the airscrew blades to a new setting.

It may be imagined that electricians

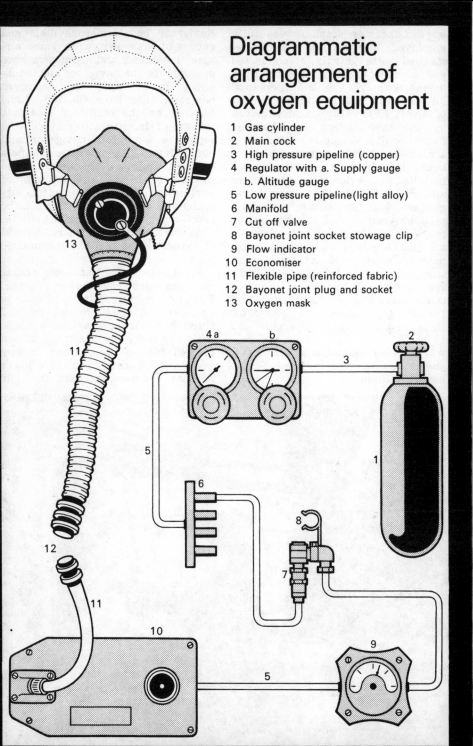

Diagrammatic arrangement of oxygen equipment

1 Gas cylinder
2 Main cock
3 High pressure pipeline (copper)
4 Regulator with a. Supply gauge
   b. Altitude gauge
5 Low pressure pipeline (light alloy)
6 Manifold
7 Cut off valve
8 Bayonet joint socket stowage clip
9 Flow indicator
10 Economiser
11 Flexible pipe (reinforced fabric)
12 Bayonet joint plug and socket
13 Oxygen mask

on a Lancaster station were fully employed. The wiring, a cynic remarked quite untruly, if connected end to end would have stretched from operating height to the sergeants' mess. Current was provided by a pair of 24-volt, 1,500-watt generators driven by the inboard engines, charging four 12-volt, 40-amp-hour batteries arranged to give 24-volts and 80-amp-hours for all services. Wiring was installed as a series of junction-boxes and conduits – like the wiring 'loom' of a car, each connection having its plug designed so that it could not be put together the wrong way. Unlike a car the Lancaster had three control panels: a main panel on the starboard side of the fuselage forward of the main spar, and panels in front of the pilot (Lancasters had left-hand drive) and the Flight Engineer on his right. Naturally the Radio Operator and

A WAAF electrician adjusts the bomb switch units just aft of the bomb-aimer's position

Navigator had numerous dials and gauges of their own, while extra airspeed indicators and altimeters were provided for the navigator and bomb-aimer. In the same way the gyro compass, hung from the top of the fuselage on the starboard side just forward of the entrance door operated repeaters for pilot, navigator and bomb-aimer. The magnetic compass was on the pilot's left, underneath the instrument board. Another case of duplication (in late production aircraft) was auxiliary steering for the bomb-aimer to use during the run in. This was arranged via the rudder and elevator servos of the automatic pilot.

From outside the Lancaster's front end bore some resemblance to a car. The pilot, ensconced in an adjustable upholstered seat looked for'ard through a windscreen like a car's, with the difference that the screen merged into a transparent canopy instead of a roof. The two lower Perspex panels were fixed in their

elektron die-cast frames, the two curved corner ones above could be opened, as on a Vintage car. The actual 'bonnet' was short, extending just far enough to cover the rudder-bar. Beyond and below were stations for the front gunner in his power-operated turret and for the bomb-aimer, whose professional activities kept him lying prone on the floor. His view forwards was excellent through the big Perspex bubble forming the nose of the aircraft, and to avoid distortion an optically flat glass pane was installed in the 'chin', angled so that targets would be properly in view during the bombing run. A glycol spray, worked by a hand pump, kept the glass free from ice. As he lay peering forward the bomb-sight 'came conveniently to eye' and the release mechanism (called by crews Mickey Mouse), electrically triggered, was beneath his right hand. In some air-craft, notably the B1 (Special) 'Dam Busters' of 617 Squadron, in which the front turret was likely to be manned

all the time, the gunner had stirrups to rest his feet on so that they did not dangle above the bomb-aimer's face.

This nose compartment was reached by one step down from the main cabin, the actual step housing a glycol tank; the cabin was higher because it formed the roof of the bomb bay. Originally Lancasters carried a Second Pilot, as in peacetime airliners, but by 1942 this requirement was dropped, mainly to save manpower, and his place was taken by a Flight Engineer. Officially the latter's main job was to monitor the pilot's throttle and pitch settings and thus calculate fuel consumption – in motorists' terms, to make sure he had not got his foot too hard on the accelerator and was not hanging on unnecessarily to low gear – but in practice the Flight Engineer was a continual help to the pilot, an extra pair of hands and an extra pair of eyes.

The Perspex nose of the Lancaster with the bombardier's flat glass pane which prevented distortion

By taking charge of throttles, airscrew pitch controls, landing flaps and undercarriage operation he left the pilot free to concentrate on the flying. During a landing approach he called out the height and speed.

Immediately behind the pilot's armoured seat sat the navigator at his table making constant calculations. Wartime navigation was far from the simplicity of airline flying. Many changes of course were needed to mislead the defences, quite apart from routine 'weaving' to avoid fighters and flak. Crossing the West Wall, or coast of Europe, in 1943 has been likened to conning a ship through a mine-field, while the low-level flying practised by special duties squadrons demanded non-stop application to large-scale roller maps so that landmarks could be identified in fitful moonlight at a speed of more than 200mph.

The clear-view blister on the canopy of Lancaster W4783

A 'clear-view' blister in the Perspex on the starboard side between pilot and navigator gave improved views forwards, astern and downwards, and there was a sliding window on each side in line with the pilot's seat, through which the navigator could scan landscape or coastline with night glasses. At the back of what we should now call the flight deck, at the extreme rear of the canopy (i.e. just forward of the mainplane front spar) was a blister in the roof called the astrodome, giving a clearish view of the sky in all directions and affording rare opportunities for the use of a sextant. To reach the astrodome one passed the radio operator, with his complex gear, including a variety of sophisticated and ever-changing radio and radar direction-finding, navigational and target-finding devices, and the IFF providing 'Identification Friend or Foe' of neighbouring aircraft. The Avro Company explained these matters quite clearly:

'The wireless operator's seat is fixed

facing forward on the front of the front spar on the port side of the aircraft. The major portion of the wireless equipment is mounted in front of the wireless operator, on or below the navigator's table, which extends forward in front of the wireless sets. Mounted in the W/T crate is a Marconi Transmitter, T.1145 and Receiver R.1115. To the left of these wireless sets is mounted the amplifier and underneath the crystal monitor. The rotary converters are mounted one above the other underneath the table.

'At the forward end of the Navigator's table, behind the pilot's seat is mounted the TR.1335 navigator's wireless equipment with the control unit installed on the floor immediately below. Fuses for the IFF (Identification, Friend or Foe) unit and TR.1335 detonators TR. 1335 and TR.-1196 are mounted in a bakelite fusebox on the navigator's panel, port side of the navigator's table.'

The mention of detonators gives a clue to the nature of this equipment.

TR.1335 was a code name for 'Gee', a radar-grid navigational aid which will be discussed later in this book; it was hoped that the Germans, who might or might not have captured an experimental version of Gee, would be led into thinking that 'TR' stood for transmitter-receiver, and hence not investigate more closely. The ruse worked for several months, and TR.-1335 remained an RAF code name for Gee.

Another pointer to the existence of electronic equipment in the midships sector of the Lancaster was the construction of the transparent canopy over the flight deck. At the front the windscreen frames were elektron diecastings. Above the pilot's seat and beside it the framework was of welded stainless steel tubing for strength and to carry the sliding windows; but from here back to the astrodome the canopy had formers of laminated spruce, complete with blister for the Radio DF (direction finding) loop. It may be mentioned that the Lancaster had a multiple array of aerial systems for the security of the crew and the confusion of ground personnel. On the port side a trailing aerial, either abaft the bomb bay or beside the W/T operator. Also on the port side a fixed aerial running from the pilot's canopy to the top of the port fin, its lead-in going through the side of the fuselage into the wireless cabin. Sticking up above the canopy was a whip aerial. The DF loop has already been mentioned; the two wires running from the ends of the tailplane to the fuselage were for the IFF (Identification, Friend or Foe) equipment, the 'black box' for which was mounted on the port side of the fuselage abaft the midturret. A dipole aerial for the Lorenz Blind Approach system hung just aft of the bomb doors, where later machines were to wear the large blister for the H2S scanner. So much for the aerials.

Asked what was the first thing that struck him about the inside of a Lancaster one man remarked that he

37

couldn't remember, because there were so many things to knock your head on it was useless to keep count. Despite its size, the big bomber was rather cramped, being almost as full of works as a watch, the problem, as in a yacht or caravan, being to find stowage for all the odd articles 'wanted on voyage'. Aircrew entered through an access door on the starboard side just forward of the tail plane, having climbed a light portable ladder; a step on the threshold took them over the ammunition-runways leading from a magazine amidships down to 'Tail-end Charlie's' lonely outpost in

Perched on a collapsable seat next to the pilot, the flight engineer checks his instruments

the stern. At least his station was nearest to the Elsan WC, thoughtfully installed beside the door. To reach his turret he made his way past the leg of the tailwheel, spigoted into the tail plane, stepped over the tail plane spars (very little headroom here) and through some folding doors to give protection from draught and fire. A sliding door then led to the turret, past a 'dead man's handle' for centring the turret fore-and-aft so that he could be fished out in emergency.

Leaving 'Charlie' to his tail end the rest of the crew would turn right on entering the aircraft, past the racks for vacuum flasks and miscellaneous items festooning the walls, such as dip-sticks for the petrol tanks (for checking suspect gauges), a fireman's

axe, and the ammunition runways. The mid-upper gunner could then climb into his turret to check the two .303 Brownings and the lower one-gun turret, if fitted, could also be populated. There was now a step up on to the flight deck because the bomb stowage extended aft almost to the lower turret. Prominent amidships was the flare chute in the floor, used also for shovelling out 'Window', the bundles of tinfoil which bedevilled the enemy's radar. Here too were the main magazines. The walls of the fuselage were liberally hung with fire-extinguishers.

For a large man in flying kit the journey for'ard was an obstacle-race, especially when crossing the mainplane spars. The latter formed two thick steps, temporarily halving the available headroom. In the space between them was arranged a rest bunk, fore-and-aft on the port side with stowage for oxygen bottles below. Armoured doors separated this mid-section from the cabin, reached by a step over the front mainplane spar. The armoured doors gave some protection from fighter attack and also helped to restrict the spread of fire, an all-too-common excitement. Various emergency exits were provided: in the pilot's canopy, in the centre section above the rest bunk, and again in the top of the fuselage in front of the upper turret. There was

'Tail-end Charlie's' turret in the stern of Lancaster DS771

also an emergency hatch right forward, beneath the bomb-aimer's cushion, which when lifted up revealed a locking handle. These emergency exits could hardly be called accessible. A rear gunner had simply to rotate his turret, open the sliding doors and fall away backwards, provided of course that his parachute was present and intact. Any parachutes not being worn – for example, by navigator, bomb-aimer, wireless operator or flight engineer – were stowed at the end of the navigator's table close to some more oxygen bottles.

The floor surface was light-alloy sheet embossed with a diamond pattern to provide some grip, but it became very slippery with lubricating oil and hydraulic fluid (mineral oils) after battle damage. Very precarious when the pilot was obliged to 'corkscrew' in avoiding night fighters, or when seeking an emergency exit in the face of adverse 'g'. This may have had some bearing on the lower survival rate amongst Lancaster crews compared with some of the other Heavies; on the other hand Lancasters were called upon for all the most hazardous missions and for the deepest penetration of enemy territory, as well as for a number of very low-level operations which will be mentioned elsewhere. Some astonishing stories of survival are recorded, however.

The cannon-firing Focke Wulf 190 outgunned the Lancaster which was protected only by its .303 Brownings

During a raid on Schweinfurt, fifty miles north-west of Nuremberg, on 26th April 1944, a Lancaster of 106 Squadron was attacked by a Focke-Wulf 190 which set the starboard inner Merlin on fire. The flight engineer, Warrant Officer Norman Jackson pressed the fire-extinguisher button, each engine having its own built-in extinguisher, but without lasting effect. So, as a desperate remedy for a desperate situation, he made his way up to the escape hatch in the roof beside the astrodome, turned the handle anti-clockwise to unlock it and climbed out into the 200mph slipstream. From the roof he dropped down to the wing and there, pausing with no visible means of support, made a successful grab for the air-inlet slot

in the leading edge. Then, hanging on precariously, he inserted the nozzle of a hand extinguisher through a slot in the engine cowling. This had its effect and the fire died down; but before it was completely out the enemy fighter returned and as Fred Mifflin, the Lancaster pilot, banked to avoid it the fire-extinguisher was torn from Jackson's grip and fire broke out afresh. The skipper ordered 'Abandon Ship'. Before leaving the aircraft Jackson had opened his parachute; now, when the front gunner opened his own escape hatch the chute billowed out, filling the cabin with silk.

As the Lancaster corkscrewed to avoid attack Jackson was swept from the wing and dragged through space at the end of his parachute shroud lines while Maurice Toft the bomb-aimer and the navigator Frank Higgins strove to shovel the canopy out through the hatch before themselves taking to the silk.

Suddenly Jackson found himself free and his parachute open, although glowing patches on the shroud lines and canopy where fire had taken hold were hardly reassuring. One by one these disappeared, blown out by the cold night air. Gravity, he reflected muzzily, was in his favour. It was in fact working rather too well, assisted by the tears in the canopy. Badly burned, and with shell splinters in one leg, Jackson hoped for a soft landing. Mercifully he came down on some bushes which cushioned his fall, although not enough to prevent one ankle being badly sprained and the other one broken. At daybreak he crawled to a cottage, where kindly hands dressed his wounds while the master of the house, anything but sympathetic to one of 'Churchill's terror flyers', went for the police Soon Norman Jackson was in a POW hospital, where he remained ten months.

After the war, when the story of his wing-walking came to be told, Warrant Officer NC Jackson of 106 Squadron was awarded the VC.

Sources of power

**Four Merlins hoist the thirty-ton
Lancaster aloft**

The four huge petrol engines which hoisted each thirty-ton Lancaster into the sky may seem archaic in the world of modern aviation, but to an automobile engineer they still seem modern enough; in fact the phrase 'overhead camshaft Vee-12, super-charged' is champagne to any motoring enthusiast. Twelve-cylinder Vee-engines are used in some of the world's finest and most powerful cars, and these run on 100-octane fuels, as developed for wartime Merlin and Hercules. Superchargers, once widely used in motor racing, are now banned from the Grand Prix circuits because cars are thought to go fast enough without them, but this method of forcing an overdose of fuel and air into the cylinders is still what makes the 'dragsters' go – those special sprint cars which will reach 200mph from rest in about one-fifth of a 2,000-yard runway. In motoring terms the Lancaster's Rolls-Royce Merlins are still quite topical.

There is of course the question of scale. A Rolls-Royce Silver Shadow car engine has a cubic capacity of 6¼ litres, a Cadillac Eldorado a little more than 8. The Merlin had 27 litres, but in general arrangement it was very similar to the twelve-cylinder excitements offered by Ferrari, Lamborghini and Jaguar, although in the fashion of its time the Merlin's bore/stroke ratio was under square (137.1 by 152.4 millimetres or 5.4 by 6 inches), and to eliminate all possibility of gasket trouble, the cylinder-heads

were non-detachable as in Bugatti, Bentley and other Vintage cars. Each bank was a one-piece casting in RR 50 aluminium alloy comprising heads and coolant-jackets into which the six high-carbon steel wet liners were inserted, with special valve-seats screwed into the heads – aluminium-bronze for inlet, silichrome for exhaust. Valve-guides were cast-iron and phosphor-bronze respectively, and the pistons were light-alloy forgings in RR 59. It will surprise no one interested in racing engines to learn that the valves were all made from heat-resisting KE 965 steel, four to each cylinder disposed on the axis of the bores, the inlets towards the middle of the Vee, the exhausts outside. Exhaust valves were hollow and sodium-filled to get rid of the heat, with Brightray over the crown and seating surfaces, and hardened steel caps at the ends. Each block had a single overhead camshaft, gear driven, and with a rocker to each valve. There were two sparking-plugs per cylinder, with ignition by magneto.

The two banks were disposed at 60 degrees, as in almost all Vee twelves, and the crankshaft was a chrome-molybdenum steel forging, nitrogen hardened, and with integral balance weights. Each crankpin carried two connecting rods of H section, forged from nickel steel – one plain and one forked, the forked one having a nickel-steel bearing-block lined inside and out with lead-bronze. Wartime rumour stated that until Packards got into production there was only one shop in the world making Merlin crankshafts. It is to be hoped rumour was wrong; certainly it was a complex operation. Main bearings, having split mild steel shells, lead-bronze lined, were carried in the upper half of the crankcase, which also took part of the airscrew reduction-gearing. There was a torsional damper shaft to drive the auxiliaries; but what proclaimed most loudly the Rolls-Royce origins of the Merlin was the 'wheelcase' – which in lesser circles would have been known as a timing cover – housing the drives for camshafts, magnetos, pumps for coolant, and oil, and supercharger, as well as the hand and electric starters and a generator to keep the batteries charged. This 'wheelcase', like the rear-axle casing of FH Royce's first great success, the Silver Ghost car of 1906, was held – one might almost say stitched – together by a ring of closely spaced bolts. In later, high-altitude fighter Marks of the Merlin, the intercooler between the primary and secondary superchargers was also mounted here.

The first make of carburetter used on the Merlin was an SU/Rolls-Royce bearing a family resemblance to the SU carburetters fitted to many prewar sports models and to the majority of present day British Leyland cars. It was a twin-choke updraught instrument with automatic and two-position mixture-control device; one jet controlled by aneroid (arranged to fail safe in the rich position) and another by aneroid subject to boost pressure. The carburetter was coolant-jacketed against freezing and the return coolant was led through the hollow throttle valves. Early Marks of Merlin used during the Battle of Britain had brought trouble to fighter pilots by cutting out when confronted with negative 'g'; a sudden dive made the fuel supply momentarily dry up. This was of less consequence on bombers, of course, and the trouble did not occur on later Marks, nor with the Bendix-Stromberg carburetters fitted to Packard Merlins in the Lancaster III and Lancaster X.

To increase power for take-off and to maintain it at high altitudes where the air contains less oxygen all Lancasters were fitted with supercharged engines. The supercharger was merely a very high-speed centrifugal fan driven by the engine which, drawing in air from the atmosphere and past the carburettor jets where it was mixed with petrol, blew the compressed mixture into the engine, thus supplying a far denser charge of explosive gas to the cylinders than the pistons could have sucked in unaided. The Merlin XX had a two-speed 'blower', as the supercharger was often called, the change-speed mechanism being operated by oil pressure from the scavenge pump of the engine. An ingenious automatic servo device was connected to the throttle – the lever equivalent to a car's accelerator pedal – to ensure the correct boost pressure for any throttle opening.

Mention of a scavenge pump will have already suggested that the Merlin had dry sump lubrication, i.e. that oil was kept not in the crankcase as in most motorcars, but in tanks in the wings from which it was circulated at high pressure by a number of pumps.

It could hardly be otherwise when the oil tank housed behind each engine contained 37½ gallons of oil. This included two gallons needed for feathering or changing the pitch of the Rotol or De Havilland constant-speed airscrews, which was done by means of oil pressure. In propeller-driven aircraft a coarse pitch setting of the airscrew corresponds to the high gear of a car, used for cruising, while fine pitch is equivalent to the lower gears used for climbing and acceleration. Feathering an airscrew meant turning the blade edgeways, as an oarsman 'feathers' his oar, to present the least possible air-resistance when for any

The Bentley engine of 1928 with its supercharger

Rolls-Royce Merlin engine

reason an engine was stopped in flight.

Of course the engines in a Lancaster had many jobs to do besides driving the aeroplane. They drove air-compressor pumps, a vacuum pump, a complex system of pumps for the hydraulically operated landing-flaps and gun turrets, and an electric generator or dynamo to charge the four 12-volt batteries for running the electrical services in flight. On the ground 'slave' batteries were plugged in to conserve the aircraft's own current, and although it was possible to start all four engines 'on the batteries' this was not recommended. Starting in cold weather was quite a problem in the days before multi-grade oils but a Ki-Gas priming pump injected rich mixture into the cylinders (as on the more recalcitrant types of big Vintage car) and in addition there was what now seems the barbarous expedient known as Worth oil dilution. After the oil tanks had been topped up after a

flight and before the engines had fully cooled down a switch in the pilot's cockpit was pressed, admitting petrol from the fuel lines into the oil pipes just before the main oil pump, thus reducing the viscosity of the oil enough to allow a cold start. As the engine warmed up this petrol evaporated.

A radiator was mounted below the engine in each nacelle, slightly pressurised to raise the boiling point as in a modern car, and containing between eleven and twelve and a half imperial gallons. The coolant was a 70/30 mixture of water and ethylene glycol to prevent boiling at high altitudes and freezing on the ground in winter, and the operating temperature was controlled by electro-pneumatically operated radiator shutters with appropriate gauge and switch for the flight engineer. Each nacelle had its built-in fire extinguisher.

A bullet in a Merlin radiator spelled real trouble: overheating, seizure and

possibly fire. Mark II Lancasters gave no such anxieties because their Bristol Hercules engines were air cooled. No radiators. The fourteen finned cylinders were arranged radially like the spokes of a wheel in two banks, slightly staggered to improve cooling, and the fact that the Hercules had Burt McCullum sleeve valves was obvious from its small diameter and neat appearance. No overhead valve-gear to maintain, no tappets to adjust, fewer inertia loadings. Inside, the engine was free from local hot-spots and so would accept higher compression ratios before detonation set in. Sleeve valves were also more tolerant of highly leaded wartime 100 octane fuels, and Bristols claimed better fuel and oil consumption and lower manifold temperatures.

There is no motorcar equivalent nowadays of the single-sleeve valve although it was used in the late 1920s by the firm of Arroll-Aster, and Barr & Stroud made a motorcycle on the same

Avro Lancaster Mk II prototype in December 1941

principle, which was simple: a single reciprocating and oscillating sleeve in each cylinder, driven at half engine speed and uncovering inlet and exhaust ports in the cylinder walls. The Hercules sat neatly in its circular cowling provided with adjustable cooling gills controlled electrically from the flight engineer's panel. A two-speed centrifugal supercharger was driven from a torsion shaft splined into the back of the crankshaft and all the auxiliaries were neatly hung on the bulkhead behind. It was of course a static radial not a rotary like the Le Rhônes and Clergets of the First World War; the cylinders and crankcase remained stationary while the crankshaft rotated, driven round by one master connecting rod per bank having six identical 'slave' connecting rods articulated to it in bearings arranged around the periphery of the big end.

49

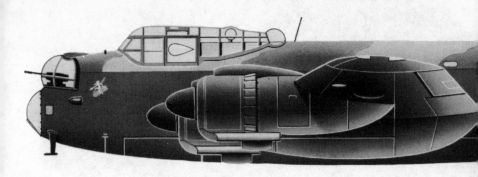

The Avro Lancaster II (B II in squadron service) differed from the Mk I in being powered by Bristol Hercules radial engines in place of the Merlins of the Mk I. This change was made as it was feared that demand for the Merlin might outstrip the supply. All Lancaster IIs were built by Armstrong Whitworth at Bagington from September 1942 onwards. The prototype, DT810, had flown for the first time on 21st September, 1941. The aircraft illustrated is DS626, flown by Sergeant G P Finnerty of the Royal Canadian Air Force with No 115 Squadron from East Wretham

The Beaufighter or 'Whispering Death', major user of the Bristol Hercules engine

in March 1943. The first Lancaster II to bomb Germany had done so on 16th January, 1943. *Engines:* Four Bristol Hercules VI or XVI radials, 1,735hp each. *Crew:* 7 except on low level missions when an 8th crew member was carried to operate the ventral gun. *Speed:* 270mph at 16,000 feet. Other performance figures: As standard Mk I. *Armament:* Standard Mk I except bomb load of up to 23,095lbs. *Weight empty/ loaded:* 36,449/63,000lbs. *Dimensions:* As standard Mk I

With a bore and stroke of 5¾-in by 6½-in (146 × 165mm) the Hercules had a capacity of 38·7 litres to the Merlin's 27 litres and gave more power at low altitudes. This was one reason that Mark II Lancasters all had bomb doors big enough to accommodate an 8,000 lb bomb.

The air-cooled Lancasters' first operation was a raid on Berlin by a flight from 61 Squadron. The first squadron operation came on 29th March 1943, another Berlin attack, by 115 Squadron, 3 Group. Mark IIs were issued also to 514 Squadron of 3 Group, but it became policy to use them mainly in Group 6, the Canadian Group, whose other aircraft were Halifaxes, which flew with the same Bristol engines. Mark II squadrons included 408, 426 and 432.

Gradually, as supplies of Packard built Merlins came through, the scare which had bred Mark IIs died down, so that by 1st August 1944, the month of Bomber Command's peak strength, only one Mark II Lancaster squadron

remained on the books, 408 (Canadian). All other Marks employed Rolls-Royce Merlin engines of one sort or another, details of which are given elsewhere. It was perhaps as well that not more than 300 Mark IIs were built, because Bristol Hercules engines were urgently needed for other uses – not only for Bomber Command's Halifax and Stirling bombers, but for the Bristol Beaufighter, Britain's very successful night-fighting aeroplane which scored many kills over England, and was responsible for useful escort and intruder operations in 1944 and 1945. It was the large, lazy slow-turning Hercules which earned the 'Beau' its nickname, in the Far East, of 'Whispering Death'. The airscrews, as on some Merlins, were variable-pitch constant-speed Rotols with electric control.

But long before this – before even Mark II had been mooted, Rolls-Royce Lancasters went into action, not only as night bombers, but in daylight.

Daylight demonstrations

A Lancaster in a daylight bombing role

On Christmas Eve 1941, when the first three operational Lancasters reached 44 (Rhodesian) Squadron, Bomber Command had high hopes that the big new bomber, faster and handier than the Halifax and Stirling which had preceded it into service, might do something about the melancholy record of misapplied bombs. The bombs themselves, reasonably to be described as bankrupt prewar stock as a later chapter will show, often failed to go off and when they did, as a gloomy survey by the Operations Research Section, Bomber Command, had established, few of them struck within miles of their destination. During the year from May 1940 until May 1941, for example, 49 per cent of the bombs 'exported' (Air Marshal Sir Robert Saundby's word) fell in open country, and on a typical sortie at the start of that period (15th—16th May 1940) only twenty-four out of ninety-six crews on the raid could establish that they had even found the target. Bomber Command, and the British public, required a shot in the arm. Germany, of course, required one elsewhere.

These shots came from two separate quarters: A V Roe and Company, whose trouble-shooting teams managed in a few short months to get most of the bugs out of the Lancaster, and High Wycombe, Headquarters of Bomber Command to which Air Marshal Sir Arthur Harris was in February 1942 appointed C-in-C. Harris believed, and said so loud and clear, that in

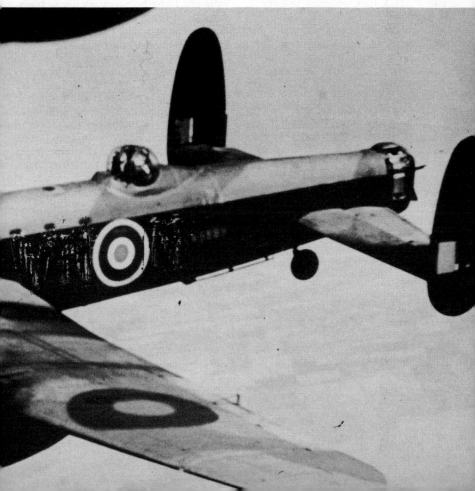

bomber aircraft lay our only hope of winning and perhaps even surviving the war. By mine-laying we could and did keep German surface vessels in harbour, except for a few brief forays, and by bombing German towns we pinned down great quantities of equipment and manpower which could otherwise have been used offensively against us. Harris was not 'shooting a line'. In 1925-26 his squadron, No 58, had put in more night flying than all the rest of the world's air forces put together. When his Hampdens in 1941 'a most feebly armed aircraft' needed better gun turrets Harris personally found a firm to design and make them on his own authority. He ordered two thousand, and when asked why so many, gave a typically pugnacious answer: 'If I had ordered twenty or two hundred I should have had to pay for them myself. And anyway they were necessary.' In the new Avro Harris knew he had a splendid night-bombing tool, far better than the Handley-Page Hampden, Short Stirling or Handley-Page Halifax.

Ironically the Lancaster's first big expedition was a daylight raid. There were strong economic-political reasons for the raid. President Roosevelt, whose country had recently entered

Messerschmitt 109s

the war, was alarmed at the shipping losses in the Atlantic and urged Churchill to do something about it. The MAN works at Augsburg in Bavaria were believed to be building over half the diesel engines used by large U-boats while cruising on the surface, as well as quantities of diesels for both transport and industrial purposes. An attack on MAN would therefore placate the Americans and help the general war effort. Harris did not like such *ad hoc* raids — oddly known then as 'panacea' targets - but he agreed to this one. On 17th April, after a week of long-distance training, six crews each from 44 and 97 Squadrons found themselves briefed to raid this factory thirty miles north-west of Munich. This meant flying some 500 miles out and home over enemy territory and at very low level.

A diversion in the Pas de Calais with thirty Boston bombers and large quantities of fighters was supposed to draw German defenders away from the Lancasters as they crossed the coast west of Le Havre, but it did not work out that way. The six from 44 Squadron led by Squadron Leader John Nettleton, a South African from Natal, were intercepted by Messerschmitt 109 and FW 190 fighters returning from the diversion, and four aircraft were quickly shot down, their archaic

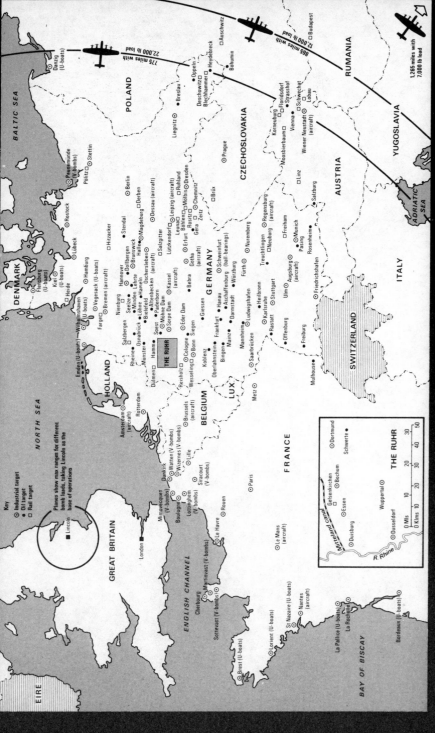

The major Allied bombing targets in Europe 1942/1945. Also shown are the ranges of Lancasters for different bomb loads

Above: Air Chief Marshal Sir Charles Portal. *Left:* Prime Minister Winston Churchill in the uniform of Air Commodore of the Royal Air Force

.303 Brownings outgunned and outranged by the German fighters' cannon. By Evreux in Normandy the fighters had dropped behind, but none of Nettleton's guns would still fire. He and his number two, Flying Officer John Garwell, pressed on alone across France to their first landmark, Lake Constance, then on to the Ammersee and thence hugging the ground, over the hills to Augsburg, where the big factory made an obvious target, unsuspecting but well defended. Well briefed on what to look for, they identified the U-boat engine shop and both aircraft dropped their four 1,000 pound bombs, observing a highly satisfactory effect eleven seconds later when the delay-action fuses went off. By this time Garwell's machine was on fire; he and three of his crew survived the forced landing.

The attack had been planned for dusk so that crews would have the benefit of darkness on the homeward run. The first of two vics from 97 Squadron arrived to bomb at roof-top height just as Nettleton, alone and unarmed, left for home. Fully awake now the defences sent heavy Flak after the three Lancasters as they left at 'nought feet' having dropped their bombs. The first machine was set on fire, and was seen to explode on hitting the ground at full flying speed. Miraculously, the pilot, Squadron Leader Sherwood, was thrown clear and escaped almost unharmed. He was the only one. The final section then made their run, heading into a full-scale barrage. No 3 aircraft was set on fire, but the pilot, Warrant Officer Mycock, DFC, held on course when he could have force-landed, and dropped his bombs before the inevitable happened and his aircraft blew up. No 2, Flying Officer Deverill, had smoke and flames pouring from the starboard inner engine, but pressed on all the same. The Germans claimed to have shot this machine down; but the crew managed to master a serious fire and the Lancaster thus early in its career showed that it could fly home on three engines. This machine, like Nettleton's and that of the section leader, Flight Lieutenant Penman, arrived back at base with all guns out of action. It had been a gallant but costly business. Squadron Leader Nettleton richly deserved his VC.

Noses were out of joint following the Augsburg raid, causing a richly comic exchange of minutes between Lord Selborne, Minister of Economic Warfare, Mr Churchill, Air Chief Marshal Sir Charles Portal, Chief of Air Staff, and Sir Arthur Harris. They began when Lord Selborne complained to the PM that his Ministry had been insufficiently consulted by Bomber Command, that there were more important targets than Augsburg and better things to bomb than diesel engines, such as ball-bearing factories at Schweinfurt, and engine works at Stuttgart. On being shown Selborne's letter Portal pointed out that the Ministry had in fact been consulted ('We have a section of Air Intelligence officers bedded out with the MEW'); but the value of the target was not the only consideration. The aim had been to assist in the Battle of the Atlantic by destroying U-boat engines, and also, by penetrating south as far as possible, to minimise opposition to Nettleton's force while at the same time causing demands for Flak from the widest possible area. The MAN works had been chosen because they were compact, unmistakeable, and readily damaged by a small force. Good landmarks made Augsburg easy to find. The raid had been successful.

The Minister was not comforted. Assisting in the Battle of the Atlantic, he rejoined, was the concern of the Defence Committee of the Air Staff, not that of the AOC-in-C Bomber Command. As to the amount of damage caused, this could be measured better by his Ministry than by the RAF. Rather wearily, Churchill initialled the following reply: 'I see these officers at least every week. We often talk these things over together; and the President has particularly asked for efforts to cut off the U-boat supply'.

After drafting this minute, the Prime Minister received a letter on the subject from 'Bomber' Harris. The Minister of Economic Warfare, Harris pointed out, had allowed no weight to the other, and essential factors which strategy, tactics and technicalities brought to bear on such an operation. They were necessarily unknown to him. These essential factors were: firstly, to make the enemy retain and exercise in Northern France a major part of his

Fighter Force, to the relief of the Russian and other fronts. (This necessitated an attack deep into France, to disabuse him of the idea that a mere defensive crust on the coast was enough.); secondly, to force the Boche to spread his air and anti-aircraft defences all over the Continent, to the extreme north and the extreme south, into France and all over the interior of Germany, thus weakening the great AA concentrations over the Ruhr, principal target of the RAF; thirdly, to go in where Fighter Command could offer some protection.

Fourthly, the target had to be attacked in daylight, but with cover shortly thereafter by darkness before bombers entered any heavily defended areas of Germany on the return journey. Fifthly, the choice of Augsburg was good from a low-level navigation point of view, because of Lake Constance and the Ammersee; but embarrassing for the enemy, who would be kept guessing until the last minute whether Augsburg, Nuremberg or Munich was the target, Munich being 'a likely objective and always a sore point with him'. An attack on Schweinfurt would have meant returning in daylight through the worst of the Flak areas, which would have required flying at high altitude – 'and the higher you go the longer daylight persists'.

The Minister must not think, Harris went on, that Bomber Command was not going after other diesel engine targets. In each of the many attacks

Above: An AA gun mounted on an Sd Kfz7 semitrack. *Left:* A light German AA gun

made on Cologne a special force was always told off to raid the Deutz suburb wherein was the second important submarine diesel engine and accumulator factory – Humboldt Deutz & Hagen. At Kiel special efforts were made to plaster the Germania works, third important diesel factory.

As to Schweinfurt, that place was as difficult to find, by day or by night, as anywhere in Germany, and Harris had satisfied himself that a ball-bearing factory was not susceptible to serious damage from a light raid. He had been to the trouble of sending an Engineer Intelligence officer round a

British ball-bearings works to weigh up the prospects. These were not good: bearings were made on batteries of multiple machines and there was no vulnerable 'bottleneck' in production. Heavy bombing would therefore be necessary.

Stuttgart was so heavily defended as to be completely out of court for a daylight raid. 'We shall go to Stuttgart (by night)' concluded Harris, 'when we can, sending half the force upon Robert Bosch AG' – the main supplier of electrical goods and diesel injector pumps.

This note, received in the afternoon

A Lancaster tests its engines before the night mission to Stuttgart

of 3rd May, Churchill forwarded to Lord Selborne with a characteristic minute which is worth quoting: 'I would suggest you take him out to luncheon one day, and have a talk with him. This would knit afresh the close relations between the two Departments. WSC.'

So much for the political aftermath of Augsburg, interesting because it shows what went on behind the scenes. Tactically, too, the raid proved valuable. It had been a mistake for successive waves to approach from the same direction, and if two or more machines could have attacked simultaneously from different quarters the AA defences would have been disorganised and confused.

Despite the casualty rate on the Augsburg raid Lancasters were sent on a number of other daylight sorties, in addition to many U-boat patrols by both Coastal and Bomber Commands. There was for example the raid of 11th July 1942 by forty of 5 Group's Lancasters from 83, 97, 106 and 207 Squadrons on a submarine-building yard at Danzig which was planned as a low-

The wooden de Havilland Mosquito takes over the daylight bombing role from the Lancaster

level daylight attack but turned into an abortive night raid in which many bombs were jettisoned and three machines lost. As a contrast came the attack (17th October) on the Schneider arms factory at Le Creusot, down on the Swiss frontier of France. In this, code-named 'Robinson' the RAF's entire force of Lancasters was com-

Arado 95w seaplane. Two were victims of 49 Squadron's Lancasters

mitted, flying out into the Atlantic over Penzance and then turning sharply inland to skim at 300 feet across the breadth of France: ninety-three aircraft from 9, 44, 49, 50, 57, 61, 97, 106 and 207 Squadrons led by Wing Commander L C Slee of 49 Squadron.

By taking this southerly route they avoided German fighters and reached the great Schneider arsenal, some 287 acres of military target, to drop their bombs at 6.09pm, with a simultaneous

attack by aircraft of 106 under Guy Gibson on a generating and transformer station at Montchanin. One Lancaster was seen to crash here. Another, limping home with engine trouble, turned fighter near Brest and shot down two out of three attacking Arado seaplanes.

Even the Alps were not a barrier to daylight operations, for apart from a number of night sorties some sixty Lancasters raided Milan on 24th October. Escorted over the Channel by Spitfires, the bombers then dispersed and proceeded to drive across France at a few hundred feet. On 6th November it was Osnabrück that received a daylight visitation, again without heavy loss. Fortunately, as De Havilland Mosquitos came into service daylight operations were handed over to them and the Lancaster was free to concentrate on its real job of night bombing.

Hitting and hitting back

A 4,000-pounder and a cluster of incendiaries over Duisburg

The offensive armaments of the Lancaster were like the presents at a fashionable wedding, both numerous and costly, and bomb-loads of a rich diversity could be made up to suit various targets. Slips to carry the bombs and their electrical fusing and release gear were built into the structure of the fuselage floor: twelve slips equally disposed in four rows of three in the forward and after sections of the floor, with two larger slips in the centre with a special firing unit and crutching gear for carrying a 4,000-lb or 8,000-lb bomb. Bombs were towed out to the aircraft on special trolleys by Waafs driving tractors, and winched into position, except in the special case of the Barnes Wallis 'dam-buster' spinning bomb, when the tail of the aeroplane was lifted by a Cole crane and the bomb trundled into position from behind.

Fortunately for the enemy British bombs were at first less efficient than British bombers. In 1939 the RAF had nothing bigger than 250 and 500 pounders of almost untested design and highly uncertain performance. These had little more than half the 'capacity' (charge to weight ratio) of German bombs and a failure rate of 30 and even 40 per cent – facts which may partly explain the official fondness for dropping leaflets instead of high explosive. Armament officers were relieved therefore when an

1,000-pound bombs are loaded into the bomb-bay

effective Medium Capacity 1,000-lb general purpose bomb was introduced in the spring of 1943, in time for the Lancaster's hey-day. It was an immediate success, and new explosives, including RDX, developed by the Research Department, Woolwich, superseded Amtol (TNT plus ammonium nitrate) and Baratol (TNT plus barium nitrate). In 1944 200,000 of the 1,000-pounders were dropped and demand exceeded supply. They were especially useful against tactical targets.

During the London blitz the Germans employed mixed loads of High Capacity (blast) bombs and incendiaries. Fortunately the raids never reached saturation point, and a catastrophic casualty rate amongst returning bombers, combined with the inexplicable attack on Russia led to the raids being called off.

Isolated bombs do little damage and small fires are easily put out. This lesson was learned by the RAF, whose Commander in Chief, Air Marshal Harris, inherited a policy of area bombardment analogous to the Coventry and London bombings when he took over from Air Marshal Sir Richard Peirse in February 1942. His most effective recipe, first seen to maximum effect in Operation *Gomorrah*, the series of raids on Hamburg in July 1943, was to combine High Capacity bombs and incendiaries. By blowing off roofs and shattering windows and doors the blast bombs created the powerful draught necessary to spread the fires from countless incendiaries. German ARP and fire services were alert but the fire reached its height in under an hour and the area devastated after three nights of raiding measured 5½ by 4 kilometres, or about ten times the area of the City of London. The intense heat generated tremendous air currents and gave rise to a firestorm previously exceeded in history only by the fire at Tokyo following the earthquake of 1923. It set a pattern for the holocaust of Dresden in 1945.

Harris forced through the design of 4,000, 8,000 and 12,000-pound blast bombs ('cookies' to bomber crews, 'block-busters' to Fleet Street) in face of Air Ministry opposition. These high capacity bombs were disliked not only by those on the receiving end. They were very fragile and hence sometimes

Above: Air Marshal Sir Richard Peirse.
Right: A 'block-buster' 12,000-pound bomb before a shrouded Lancaster

fitted with parachutes, as German 'land mines' had been, to prevent the casing breaking up or the fuse being crushed on impact. With parachute they could be nothing but an 'area' weapon, and even without the silken tail their ballistics were extremely poor. The 8,000-pound bombs were made by bolting together two 4,000-pounders and three of these were joined to make one 12,000-pounder, a weapon, as its designer, Air Commodore P Huskinson, CBE, MC and Bar, remarked, 'of almost nightmare complexity'. Three-quarters of the bomb's weight was high explosive, and after a new tail had been developed for it, the 12,000-pounder became capable of some precision. On 8th February 1944 a small force of Lancasters raiding an aero-engine works at Limoges found a factory consisting of nine large buildings, all in bays; they left it with half the bays obliterated, the rest badly shattered.

As early as spring 1941, Dr N Barnes Wallis, Controller of Armament Research at Vickers-Armstrong, realised the need for another type of high capacity bomb. The basic resources of a country, its mines and oil-fields, lie mainly below the surface, beyond the reach of ordinary bombs, and there are many other structures such as viaducts, gun-emplacements and dockyards which are too tough or too open to be damaged by any normal category of bomb, whether high capacity, general purpose, anti-personnel or armour-piercing. Accordingly Dr Wallis, designer also of the dam-busters' weapon, planned a marriage between the high capacity and armour-piercing types. This was to be a ten-ton missile containing six or seven tons of high explosive wrapped in a slender and sophisticated aerodynamic casing which would allow it to reach an extremely high terminal velocity. If released from 40,000 feet, he calculated, such a bomb would penetrate 135 feet of sand. Sliding in like a stiletto, it would then, after any desired delay, explode subterraneously, causing an earthquake tremor and literally pulling the ground away from under the target. This was the bomb eventually produced and called 'Grand Slam'. In 1941 such thinking was strictly Volume

Two. No aeroplane then existing could carry a bomb 25 feet 6 inches long and 46 inches in diameter, but a scaled down version was put in hand by the English Steel Corporation, of Sheffield. The result was 'Tallboy', a slim 12,000-pound missile 21 feet 6 inches in length and 38 inches in diameter which would fit into a suitably modified Lancaster and what is more go with it to maximum range. Tallboy was dropped successfully upon the Saumur railway tunnel in June 1943 and Tallboys were ordered *ad lib* with the battleship Tirpitz especially in view.

Intelligence reports of V-weapon sites and the discovery during the Allied advance across France of concrete structures with both roof and walls some twenty-two feet thick caused Grand Slam to be dusted off and put into production. Its big moment came in February 1945 when it toppled the Bielefeld viaduct. Grand

Streamlined 12,000-pound 'Tallboy' which was used successfully against the Saumur railway tunnel and later the *Tirpitz*

Slam reach a velocity of 1,000 feet per second (680mph) when dropped from 20,000 feet although, records Huskinson sadly, 'postwar reports of Grand Slam and Tallboy showed that their trajectory and penetration were still unsatisfactory.' However, Grand Slam remains the ultimate in non-nuclear weapons.

Incendiary bombs played as large a part as high explosives. Early Marks of incendiary tended to break up or fail to ignite. Also the method of loading by Small Bomb Containers (SBC) was both tedious and inaccurate. Later four-pound magnesium incendiary bombs of hexagonal section for easy packing were put up in clusters inside containers of 350, 500 or 1,000 pounds having reasonable ballistics, set to explode either on impact or above the target. High explosive canisters were mixed with incendiaries to discourage the defence. Liquid-filled 30-pound 'J' bombs were pressed upon Bomber Command in 1944. These often failed and their contents, as Harris gleefully pointed out, were warmly welcomed by the enemy as *ersatz* motor spirit.

The firework display over Germany was enlivened by a number of Target Indicators, used mainly by Lancasters and Mosquitos of the Pathfinder Force, inaugurated in August 1942. There were several types of TI from 250 pounds to the model weighing 2,300 pounds which made use of a 4,000-pound bomb casing. This was the Pathfinders' 'Pink Pansy' in which a red pyrotechnic was added to the basic marker mixture of benzole, rubber and phosphorus. There were also TI bombs of good ballistic form arranged to eject coloured roman candles either in the air or on impact, with or without explosives. A 250-pound TI lit up a radius of 100 yards. Sometimes parachute flares and reconnaissance flares were used, launched down the chute amidships, which was also the exit for bundles of 'Window' foil used in baffling the enemy's radar.

With these and other items the Lancaster's offensive arsenal was fairly comprehensive, but defensive armament was poor, being for the most part limited to Colt-built Browning machine guns taking the standard British army .303 rimmed cartridge of virtually First World War pattern. It needed 'a great amount of .303 ammunition, very accurately aimed, to pierce the armour of a 109' said one fighter pilot and the bomber boys could echo this most fervently, having at the most four guns firing from a single aiming point. Best armed of the Lancaster's gunners was 'tail-end Charlie', whose FN 20 turret had four Brownings. The FN 5 nose turret packed two guns, as did the FN 50 mid-upper. The FN 64 ventral turret, when fitted, carried one Browning only, or a Vickers K gun – a reincarnation of the old drum-feed Lewis. As the initials suggest, all turrets were designed by one Captain Archie Frazer-Nash, whose chain-drive sports cars had so enlivened motoring competitions during the 1920s. Power for rotating the turrets was hydraulic. They functioned very much like the servo steering of a car, without conscious effort on the part of the gunner, who had only to squeeze master grips on the gun handles to obtain slow or fast

'Grand Slam' 22,000 pounds and still the ultimate in non-nuclear weapons

Part of the arsenal available to the Lancaster

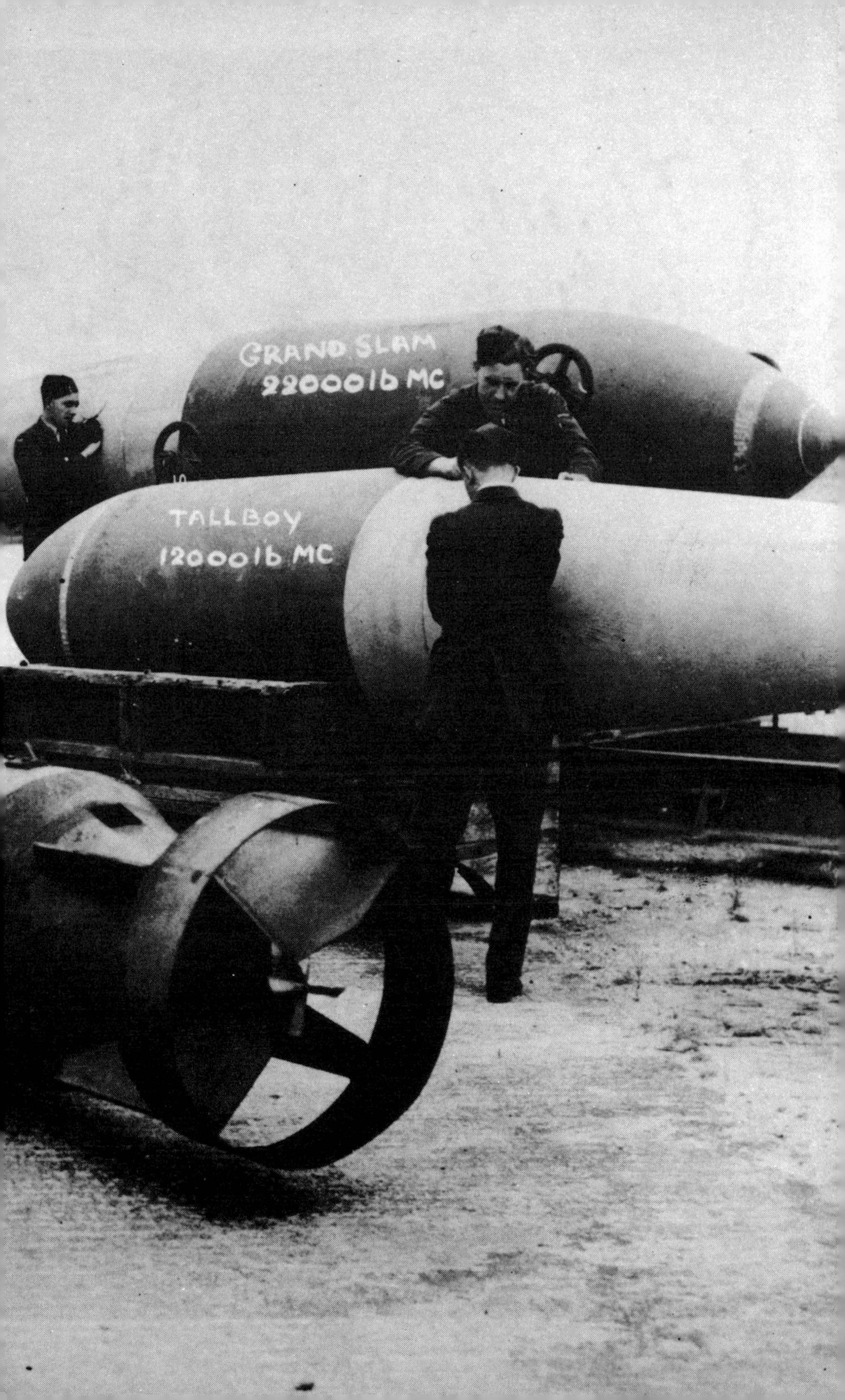
GRAND SLAM
22000 lb MC
TALLBOY
12000 lb MC

otation. The mid-upper turret was
nanned constantly as a lookout, the
ront only occasionally. Tail gunners
vere on duty all the time, leading an
xistence that was lonely, respons-
ble, dangerous, draughty and cold.
'he problem of turret heating was
ever satisfactorily solved. Some late
roduction models were fitted with an
'N 82 tail turret carrying two .5
Browning guns, or an FN 121 having
our .303 Mark II Brownings.

The private venture turret for 5
nachine guns, energetically pursued
y Air Marshal Harris, progressed
lowly because Rose & Son of Gains-
orough had no facilities for mass
roduction. Each was virtually a one-
ff job. Ironically, if America had not
ntered the war Bomber Command
vould have had half-inch machine
uns in 1941. Four factories to manu-
acture them had been set up in the
Jnited States by the Ministry of Air-
raft Production but when the US
ame in these factories were requi-
itioned by Britain's new allies.

Experiments were also made with
utomatic gun-laying turrets in 1944
vhen 'Monica', a rearward-looking
ight-fighter warning radar, was fitted
o Lancasters. The fact that the
nemy had learned to 'home' on
Monica made this idea particularly
ttractive, but the Mark I ALGT
roved susceptible to 'Window'. Mark
II was less so, and two experimental
nstallations were tried. So was an
American automatically laid turret,
ut the Lancaster finished the war
rmed in the main with the old
immed .303 round, out-ranged and
ut-gunned by cannon-firing fighters.
As it was, the bomber's best defences
vere darkness and cloud. Fortunately
s the war progressed various radar
ids, to be discussed later, enabled
hem often to operate unseen.

As, night after night, the bombers
eft England in a steady stream
nd straggled home six or more hours

later, many of them in evident dis-
tress, listeners on the ground must
have wondered about the organization
behind each raid and the physical
facts about flying over Germany.
This was not something one could
enquire about in pubs, and aircrew
would not have discussed it if asked:
'Careless talk costs lives' urged the
official posters. (A slogan sometimes
twisted into 'Careless lives cause
talk'.) Fortunately at this distance
most of the questions can be answered.

A chain of command starting with
the War Cabinet issued directives to
the Air Staff about what might and
might not be bombed; and requests for
bomber support came in from various
departments. The army, for example
before and during the invasion of
France, the Ministry of Economic
Warfare passim, Special Operations
Executive for a Mosquito attack on
Amiens gaol to free Resistance fighters, and the Royal Navy. One re-
members Harris's definition of 'Strategic objectives' – 'generally a eu-
phemism for targets chosen by the
Admiralty'.

Daily decisions on targets were
taken by HQ Bomber Command at
High Wycombe from information com-
piled by the Air Ministry, and Groups
were given their orders. Each Group
HQ did its own tactical planning, with
due consideration of its own meteor-
ological reports. The Group Commander, who was an Air Vice Marshal,
then briefed Station Commanders and
Squadron Commanders in the group
either at a conference or by discussion
on linked telephones. The 'station
master' decided which squadrons and
how many aircraft should take part.
Armament Officers then chose bomb
loads according to the type of target
and availability of bombs, and Navigation Officers assembled their navigators who worked out courses to
avoid known danger spots and to
include 'spoofs' and feint attacks as
required, to deceive the enemy.
Each Group AOC was in close touch,
during the later stages of the war,

with 100 Group, the radar specialists whose arsenal of 'electrickery' contained all manner of devices to confound the enemy's early warning, electronic gun-laying, searchlight-control, fighter control and Airborne Interception systems.

Actual briefing took place about three hours before take-off. All crews reported to the Operations Room, together with the Navigation Officer, Armament Officer, Met Officer, Squad-ron Commanders and Station Commander. The Intelligence Officer gave reasons for the operation and latest reports on defences; the Navigation Officer gave out the best heights to fly at over each part of the sortie, and the Met man talked about the weather. Then came a summing up by the Station or Squadron Commander who announced the number of aircraft taking part from other stations, discussed the importance of the raid and provided usually an alternative target.

There was no time to lie around

The navigator at work just behind the pilot's seats

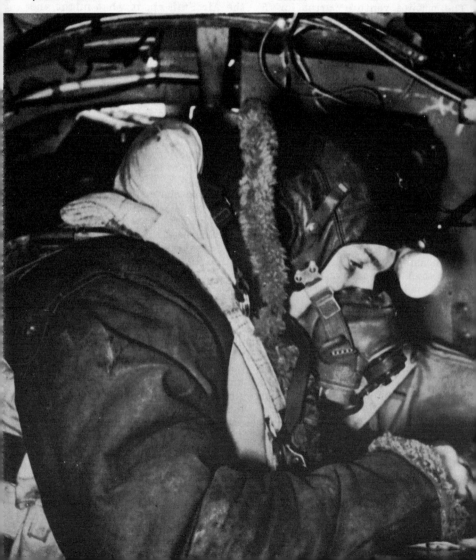

fter briefing. Each crew member had o check his own equipment: gunners hecked their guns and ammunition upplies, and wireless operators ested radio sets and made sure the ntercom was working properly. It vas then up to the captain of each ircraft (usually but not invariably he pilot) to make doubly sure that everything was OK; but he knew which crew members he could trust. Crews brought their own vacuum lasks of coffee, flight rations of chocolate, and escape kit.

The navigator plotted the course

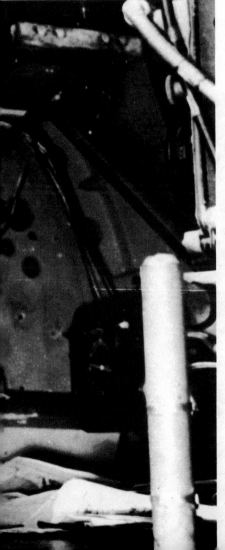

and obtained bearings from the wireless operator. He looked after 'Gee', the radar grid-reference device, and reminded the pilot about defences, searchlight belts and so on, working very closely with the wireless operator. His station was conveniently close to the astrodome for the rarish occasions when it was possible to obtain a 'fix' from stellar observation. The wireless operator had responsibility for timekeeping, which was important because operations were timed to the minute; for example any fires alight before the time the Pathfinders were due to have laid their incendiaries would probably be German decoys. He was constantly getting bearings from ground stations and checking navigational beams; also watching for recognition signals on the homeward run. He also acted as reserve gunner.

The mid-upper turret formed a sort of conning-tower which the gunner seldom left and which gave a rather more than hemispherical view. The gunner never ceased swinging his turret round, and reported his observations to the captain. A contoured 'taboo track' with interrupter gear prevented the guns from being depressed far enough to shoot away parts of the aeroplane, although a case was reported of a tail-gunner being shot from the mid-upper position – no doubt through combat damage to the track. All in all the tail gunner had the least enviable job and one of the most responsible. Trouble usually approached from astern. He was the first to see enemy fighters and it was his job to give 'an accurate and unimpassioned commentary' on the fighter's approach and how it might be evaded. In defended areas he also told the captain whether Flak was catching up or dropping behind, what time the aeroplane was 'corkscrewing' to spoil the defenders' aim. Over sea he assisted navigation by keeping his guns trained on a flare float now and again to calculate drift.

Three miles from target the bomb

aimer took over from the navigator. He had already studied target maps and possibly models very carefully. During the cliff-hanging thirty seconds run-in he gave a running commentary, having a clear view forwards and downwards through his optically flat aiming panel. In late production Lancasters the bomb aimer could even steer the aircraft himself, having controls linked to the rudder and ailerons via the automatic pilot mechanism. In OBOE aircraft, the run up to the target took ten minutes of almost straight and very accurate flying.

Three-quarters of an hour before take-off the crew bus drove crews out to their aircraft, where they again

The bomb-aimer about to operate the release button on his Mark IX bomb sight

checked things over. On large operations aircraft were lined up on th runway or taxi-ing track. When onl four or five machines were going the taxied out from dispersal. They too off at 30-second intervals, heading int the dusk so that it would be dark whe they crossed the enemy coastline.

Not all trips, fortunately, were ten tenths adventure for everyone con cerned. All around the sky might b punctuated by the quick anonymou flash of a Lancaster blowing up, or th trail of night fighters going down i flames, while individual aircraft saile impassively out and home. One suc raid on Stuttgart is described by Group Captain Alan Wheeler, a Ser vice test pilot temporarily attache to Bomber Command, who observe the operation with the calm an critical detachment he would have

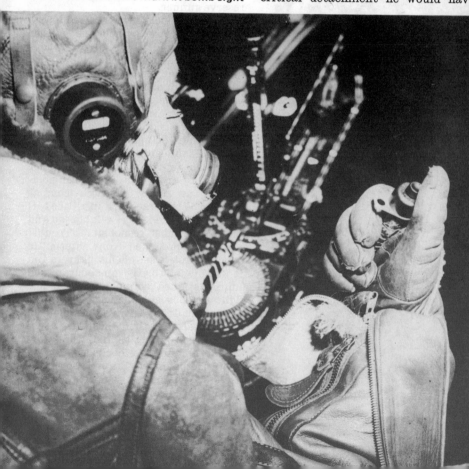

applied to his instrument readings on a simple test flight. Probably the best account of Lancaster routine, it was written for Service consumption and therefore has none of the heroics with which journalists are expected to embroider their copy. It reminds us that the normal Bomber Command crew, averaging 21 or 22 years of age, was about as introspectively neurotic as a Rugby XV.

Taking off from an East Anglian base, Wheeler's formation had reached 18,000 feet by the time they crossed the English coast. This enabled them to cross the twenty-mile-wide defence belt inside the French coast at maximum speed: an indicated 200mph representing, with the prevailing tail wind, a ground speed of 300mph as the pilot weaved thirty degrees on either side of the course to confuse the defences. Once beyond the Flak belt they lost height gradually until when passing Paris they were down almost on the 'deck', too low for Flak, below the radar line and too low for fighter interference. Any following fighter would have been washed into the ground by the bombers' slipstream.

Every thirty minutes the skipper would call up each man on the intercom for a check and for friendly relations. Casual chat was not encouraged. As the Rhine loomed up they climbed to their operational height of 12,000 feet, using cloud as cover from searchlights whenever available, but diving through it over Stuttgart. Crews could see the general outline of the town fairly well from their indicated 7,000 feet, only 5,200 feet above

German coastal Flak units

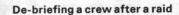

the local ground level, the river Neckar showing up fairly well in the moonlight. The bombing run was made down moon as arranged, the bomb aimer took over, gave directions and ordered 'Steady'. The skipper held straight and level for twenty seconds: at last the aircraft lifted and the word came 'Bombs gone'.

The tail gunner warned of following Flak so the skipper turned fairly sharply thirty degrees to port and dived slightly. They had dropped one 4,000-pound 'cookie' and a 4,000-pounder case of incendiaries. Coming home they crossed the Rhine at 8,000 feet and used the ensuing glide to hedgehopping level – which the Luftwaffe called '*Ritterkreuz* height' ('DSO level') – for a coffee break, opening flight-ration chocolate and reaching thermoses from the rack in the fuselage while gliding down for that exhilarating swoop across France. Then came a twenty-five minute climb back to 18,000 feet past the Kammhuber Line of Flak, searchlights and fighters, weaving or corkscrewing. Diving at 300mph they crossed the Channel at 8,000 feet, and so home to England on 'George'. The tail-gunner could now at last stand down, and as on this trip 'George' the automatic pilot proved temperamental, Wheeler took the controls, pleased to be flying a Lancaster on ops.

At the home station crews were greeted by the 'station master' and given transport to the operations room, for a mug of tea and de-briefing. Then a meal of bacon and eggs and bed. Crews were not encouraged to stay up and wait for photographs taken automatically over the target to be developed. That could keep until morning. Duration of op: 6.30pm until 3am bed-time. Thus one fairly quiet operation, as a pilot saw it. It may be contrasted with the eventful forays described in the official VC citations quoted in a later chapter.

81

Busting the dams

Buoys and anti-torpedo nets failed to
protect the Ruhr dams

It never ceases to astonish the present-day observer how quickly things were done in wartime. Less than twelve months after the Lancaster's first tentative 'gardening' exercises with 44 Squadron in March 1942 an almost outrageously novel Special was being developed. The Lancaster had proved itself the champion weight-lifter of the RAF and it was the obvious – indeed the only – choice for carrying a new kind of bomb. This bomb was the 'Scampton Steamroller' designed by Dr Barnes Wallis and the targets were hydro-electric and storage dams in the Ruhr. If these could be breached, it was realised by farsighted men on both sides, tremendous damage might be done both to industry and to civilian morale. In Germany a local dignitary wrote endless minutes to this effect, achieving nothing but unpopularity for his pains, while in England a strong dams-raid lobby grew up. The Ministry of Economic Warfare enjoyed what it called 'panacea' targets. They made it feel godlike and clever. Air Marshal Harris detested such *ad hoc* raids. Bombing, he knew, was seldom as precise as people hoped, and raids were best devoted to crippling Germany as a whole. If everything in an area could be bombed flat 'vital targets' would perish with the rest, but the Ministry's vital targets were seldom as vital as they hoped, since the Germans were brilliant at reconstruction and masters of *ersatz*. For this reason Harris refused to release a

Wing Commander Guy Gibson leads his crew aboard one of the Lancasters of 617 Squadron

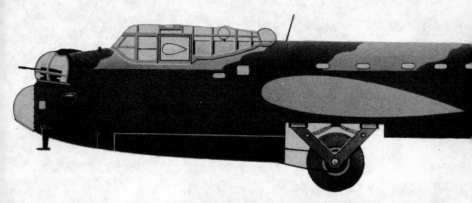

The Avro Lancaster B III (with Type 464 Provisioning) ED932 flown by Wing-Commander Guy Gibson of No 617 Squadron operating from Scampton in May 1943. This modification of the B III was designed to accommodate the dambusting bomb designed by Dr Barnes Wallis. When taken in hand for the conversion, the standard B III had the mid-upper turret removed and the hole left plated over to reduce weight and drag, the bomb bay doors removed and the bay extensively altered, and a Vickers K gun fitted in the fuselage floor. The modification to the bomb bay was to allow the fitting of two triangular supporting arms for the bomb. These were pivoted at their upper ends in the fuselage, so that the lower ends, holding the bomb, could swing away at the correct moment, allowing the bomb to drop away to the water. The bomb was mounted on spindles at the lower end of the arms, and was spun backwards at 500rpm by a belt drive from the engine of the aircraft's hydraulic system. As the machine approached the dam, with the bomb spinning backwards, a speed of 220mph and a height of 60 feet were maintained until exactly the correct range from the dam was reached and the bomb dropped. It then bounced along the surface until it hit the dam wall and sank, hugging the wall as a result of its spin, until it had reached a predetermined depth. It then exploded, setting up a shock wave big enough to rupture the wall

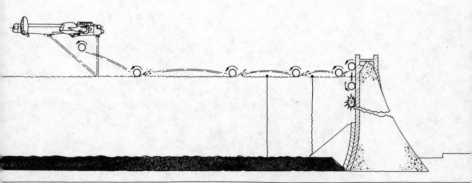

Lancaster squadron from Bomber Command to train for a special operation; instead a new unit, initially known as X Squadron, was formed with 5 Group, to be commanded by Wing Commander Guy Gibson DSO, DFC and Bar, a tough, energetic man of only twenty-five who had just completed his third tour of operations. Would Gibson, instead of going on leave, agree to make one more special trip, asked Air Vice Marshal Cochrane, AOC, 5 Group. He would, so 617 Squadron was formed at Scampton, Lincolnshire behind a dramatic curtain of secrecy.

There was every reason for this. Reconnaissance of the dams showed no barrage balloons and only light defences. The weapon which Barnes Wallis had designed worked on a completely new principle. The difficulties in attacking the dams were enormous: they lay in or just outside the Ruhr – the notorious 'Happy Valley' of Bomber Command, they were surrounded by hills, the attack would have to be made in the dark from very low level, and the dams themselves were protected by torpedo nets. Their sheer size was also extremely daunting. To topple such a structure as a demolition exercise in peacetime would have been a major engineering feat. To do so by bombing at night in enemy territory sounded virtually impossible. The Prime Minister was enthusiastic; Harris was not the only sceptic.

The operation has been described many times. Guy Gibson's own book *Enemy Coast Ahead* is a classic not only on the subject of Operation Upkeep (which for security reasons he calls 'Downwood') but also on life in Bomber Command; Paul Brickhill's *The Dam-Busters* covers the Moehne and Eder and Sorpe operations in picturesque detail and continues the history of 617 under Gibson, Leonard Cheshire, J B Tait and J E Fauquier. Both books are required reading for anyone interested in wartime flying. They are also extremely entertaining.

Barnes Wallis's bomb worked rather on the principle of 'ducks and drakes': a stone thrown spinning correctly will not plunge as soon as it touches the water but skip for some distance along the surface. This is what Group Captain Huskinson, designer of conventional bombs meant when he said that Wallis's weapon behaved in a 'remarkably unbomblike manner'. No 617 Squadron was formed at Scampton, near Lincoln, on 21st March, just twelve months after the Lancaster's first operational sallies. Time was short for training because the dams could only be attacked when they were full of water, and that season was approaching, as reconnaissance photographs showed.

So great was the secrecy that at first even Gibson himself was not told what the target was. Then he was shown models of the dams, painstakingly constructed by the Road Research Laboratory, Teddington, a department widely regarded before the war as under-employed. Dr Wallis conducted experiments with explosives and arrived at a realistic charge. A full-size but disused dam at Lake Rhayader in Radnorshire was successfully blown up after reluctant permission from Birmingham Corporation, its owners. Gibson and his new squadron of hand-picked much decorated enthusiasts practised low flying as no four-engined aircraft had ever been flown before, by night and by day, simulating moonlight by means of coloured windows and goggles. Complaints flowed in from police and citizenry which Gibson was empowered to ignore, although 5 Group HQ wrote back to one aggrieved motorist that 'in future pilots will be instructed to behave with due regard to other road users'. By day and night 617 flew courses pinpointing every lake in the United Kingdom, or thereabouts, and eventually evolved a route which simulated the courses which bombers would fly to the Ruhr, even down to canal bridges and windmills.

Meanwhile at the Avro factory work went ahead on modifications to the Lancaster, under the code name 'Type 464 Provisioning', to enable 'a certain item of stores' to be carried. At Vickers that item of stores continued to give trouble by breaking up on impact while Dr Wallis, Wing Commander Gibson and 617 Squadron's bombing leader, Flight Lieutenant Bob Hay, looked on praying that everything would be all right on the night. A final successful trial was held on 13th May 1943, three days before the actual raid.

Experiments had shown Barnes Wallis that no ordinary bomb would suffice. High level attacks would miss the target, and any bomb dropped from low level would tend to ricochet over the parapet. Torpedo attack was out because the dams were protected by nets. Only by placing an explosive charge hard up against the dam wall under water and preferably near its foundations, could an attack succeed. He calculated that about three tons of RDX, say 6,000 pounds, would do the trick.

The trick itself consisted in placing the bombs. If a bomb could be made to stay on the surface until it was over the nets then press itself against the dam face and motor down into the mud before exploding, the deed was done. At first Wallis wanted a spherical bomb because the aerodynamics of spheres were understood and predictable; but for practical reasons he settled for a drum – the 'Scampton Steamroller'.

The first modified Lancaster to reach 617, said Flight Lieutenant H B Martin, DFC of B Flight, looked more likely to walk than fly. The mid-upper turret and some of the armour had gone to save weight, the bomb doors had disappeared, leaving a sort of notch in the underbelly and the Wallis bomb, resembling an oil-drum eleven feet in diameter and mounted on trunnions, was slung beneath, held in place by triangulated callipers hinged to the sides of the bomb bay. Even so, visiting spies, had there been any at

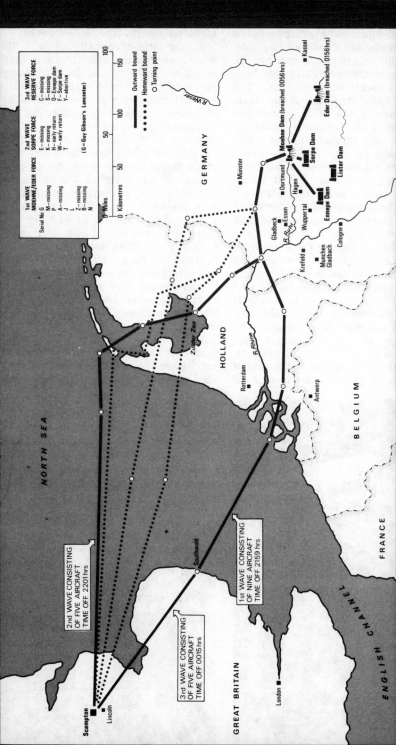

Scampton, would have been puzzled by the sprockets and chain at one side. In fact this chain drive mechanism was the principal secret of the dambusters – a secret kept until 1962. The chain and sprockets, for all the world like the final drive of a motorcycle, were rotated by the main hydraulic system of the Lancaster, and their function was to set the drum-shaped bomb spinning at a speed of 500 revolutions per minute so that it would literally 'play ducks and drakes'. Wallis had calculated that if the bomb could be released at a speed of 240mph from exactly sixty feet above the water and at a precise distance from the end of the reservoir, it would skip along the surface and hop the torpedo net. Then, pressed against the face of the dam by its momentum, and still spinning vigorously, it would roll down this wall and bury itself in the mud at the foot of the dam where, after an interval for the aircraft to fly clear, it would explode by means of a hydrostatic pistol fuse. It was an airborne automotive depth-charge.

Flying eight or more hours daily, 617 Squadron learned quickly until they could navigate in the dark by strip maps, finding their way uncannily through mountain passes to skim the surface of a lake before clearing the next summit with feet to spare. The problem of maintaining a height of exactly sixty feet over calm water in pitch darkness was solved by rigging a pair of Aldis lights whose beams converged on the surface from sixty feet precisely, and the problem of releasing the missile at exactly the right place was solved by a brilliantly simple gadget: an isosceles triangle of wood with a peep-hole at the apex and a vertical pin at each of the other corners to be lined up like a catapult on the two towers on the Moehne Dam, which were known to be 600 feet apart. Exactly one month after Roy Chadwick, Avro chief designer, signed the first works instruction, a finished prototype of the B.1 (Special) reached Farnborough for testing. On 20th

April a second prototype reached Manston for drop tests in the Thames estuary off Reculver, Kent.

So often in affairs based on Britain the weather causes postponement. This time it was perfect, and as the waters in the Ruhr reached their maximum height nineteen Lancasters left Scampton on the appointed day, 16th May, having been briefed the day before. Gibson's force was divided into three waves: one of nine aircraft under the Wing Commander himself, the others of five each. All were equipped with gadgets evolved by the crews in the last few days of training: stirrups for the air-gunner's feet to keep them away from the bomb-aimer's face – for the front turret would be manned throughout – an extra altimeter on the screen just in front of the pilot, and at Gibson's insistence the very latest VHF radio telephone equipment, as used in Fighter Command, giving clear speech at long range. They had flown 2,000 hours in training and dropped 2,500 practice bombs.

The main force under Gibson was to go straight to the Moehne and attempt to breach it by repeated bombing; it was thought that a series of shock waves under water would do the trick. They could not hope to do it in one, and the lake would have to calm down before each new attack, which meant much unhealthy loitering on site. Any bombs remaining would be dropped on Number Two target, the Eder Dam. Section Two under Flight Lieutenant Joe McCarthy would cross the enemy coast in formation as far away as possible from main force, and proceed to bomb a third dam, the Sorpe, with as much commotion as possible to

draw off enemy night fighters. The remaining five aircraft would be reserves to be called up as required.

Gibson's section flew in formation, very low – so low that one aircraft touched the sea, losing its weapon and damaging both outboard engines. Another was hit by light Flak and so badly damaged that Pilot Officer Geoffrey Rice had to return. The rest flew on along the Rhine, spared any night fighters because of their low altitude but fired at from Flak barges. Gunners returned the fire. In the Ruhr valley they flew across an uncharted German aerodrome and were caught by searchlights. Gibson broke free 'by dodging behind some tall trees' while Pilot Officer Spafford, DFM, his bomb-aimer, lying prone in the front Perspex, complained that he would soon be shaving himself on the tops of some corn in a field. Flight Lieutenant Bill Astell, slightly higher, was blinded by searchlights, and momentarily lost control. His aircraft 'reared up like a stricken horse, plunged on to the

From left to right: **The Moehne dam before the 'Scampton Steamroller'; millions of gallons of water pour through the breached Moehne dam and a thousand people died in the floods; the Eder dam, holding back 202,000,000 tons of water, also falls to Barnes Wallis's bouncing bombs**

deck and burst into flames'. Five seconds later his bomb exploded.

As Gibson's formation arrived at the Moehne, finding it defended by six 20mm light anti-aircraft guns, Joe McCarthy's outfit began staging their diversionary attack on the Sorpe dam to the south. They too had lost two machines on the way, shot by Flak after crossing the coast. As Gibson started on his run, diving to the required sixty feet above the lake, keyed to that height by the merging beams of his Aldis lamps, his companions dispersed into the hills to wait their turn. Aboard the leader's Lancaster each member of the team was keyed up to his job: gunners alert to shoot back at the Flak towers, bomb aimer glued to his special sight, and flight engineer holding the revs of each engine to the exact airspeed required, having first slowed the air-

With the dams breached vital hydro-electric power was lost to the German war effort

craft after its dive by putting on a little flap. He also stood by to pull Gibson out of his seat should he be hit. The hydraulic motor had set the Wallis bomb spinning and Spafford's hand was on the button. The bomb fell exactly on target, making the lake boil like a cauldron, weakening but not breaking the dam.

Ten minutes later when the waters had subsided Hopgood, Number Two, made his run. One hundred yards from the dam his machine was hit and set on fire. Hopgood's bomb overshot the dam but landed on the power-station beyond. Then the aircraft blew up. Next to attack was Flight Lieutenant 'Mickey' Martin, while Gibson flew in with him to draw some of the fire. Martin's machine was hit in the wing but did not catch fire. Despite the damage Martin accompanied Gibson on the latter's second diversionary run, escorting 'A Apple' flown by Squadron Leader Melvyn Young called 'Dinghy' because he had twice ditched in the Mediterranean.

Young's bomb was beautifully placed but the dam still held. Next came Flight Lieutenant David Maltby. Soon after his red Véry light had signalled 'Bomb gone' they saw that the dam was gone too. A great wall of water rushed down the valley, sweeping away buildings, bridges and communications, and flooding air-raid shelters. A thousand people died in the floods. More strategically important, the breach was draining away drinking water and hydraulic power supplies from Germany's principal industrial area. The gap the bombs had opened was almost a hundred yards wide, and sixty to seventy feet deep. Nine-tenths of the water in Moehne Lake swirled down into the valley.

Circling exultantly, Gibson called up all surviving 'Cooler' aircraft and headed for their second target, the Eder dam, whose waters lay as it were at the bottom of a bowl with sides a thousand feet high. Of the three aircraft with bombs left, Flight Lieuten-

ant David Shannon made five trial runs before pausing to sort things out. Then Gibson called up Squadron Leader Henry Maudsley in 'Z Zebra'. He too made two dives into the bowl; then a third. As his Véry curled out to signal 'bomb gone', they saw the missile hit the parapet, and the Lancaster silhouetted against the flash. Then nothing. Gibson called 'Henry, Henry, Z Zebra, Z Zebra, are you OK? Then everyone in Gibson's G George heard Maudsley's voice, very faint and far away, saying, from an apparently non-existent Lancaster, 'I think so... Stand by'. And that was all. Shannon returned to the attack. 'Back a bit, Skipper', said his bomb aimer in the classic Bomber Command joke. They went round once more. Spot on, but the dam survived. Then in went Pilot Officer L G Knight. One dummy run, and down went his bomb for a good

Mud from the Moehne dam silted-up the pumping-system from the Rhine up the Ruhr valley as far as Essen

hit. The Eder dam split with even more spectacular effect than the Moehne. Downstream, 617 knew, was a great new German training aerodrome with underground hangers and living quarters. These were going to get very wet.

Pilots detailed for the Sorpe were to make their own way. McCarthy, the big American from Brooklyn, made three dummy runs, then scored his hit. The Sorpe, made of earth holding up a watertight concrete core, was harder to shift than the sophisticated engineering of the Moehne, but the parapet was breached. McCarthy was backed up by aircraft from the reserve, Force 3. Flight Sergeant K W Brown found the lake with difficulty through the rising mist, lit himself a torch by incendiarising a pinewood, then, after no fewer than nine dummies, dropped his bomb bang on target. Anderson, the other backer-up, was beaten by mist and took his bomb home; Pilot Officer Burpee, from Canada, was shot down on the way.

Two dams remained. Pilot Officer W H T Ottley, ordered to the Lister was not heard of again; he never arrived. The last man, Flight Sergeant W C Townsend in 'O Orange', dispatched to the Ennerpe dam, searched long in the mist but found it and dropped an accurate bomb, returning via the Moehne for a last look-see. It had indeed turned out wet in the Ruhr valley.

With most of their ammunition gone and no mid-upper turrets for defence, the survivors drove home across Holland in daylight, losing 'Dinghy' Young over the sea. He had ditched for the last time. The cost of the raids had been high. Including the two which turned back after damage on the way out, ten Lancasters out of nineteen had been lost. Eight crack crews out of nineteen – fifty-six men – were posted 'missing, believed killed', and of these only three parachuted to the relative safety of a POW camp.

But three important dams had been breached. Throughout the crucial summer of 1943 while Germany was dependent on Ruhr factories for munitions on two fronts, water for industry was rationed and hydro-electric power short. Mud from the broken Moehne silted up the pumping-system from the Rhine up the Ruhr valley as far as Essen, and the dam itself was repaired only just in time to catch the autumn rains. Had the Sorpe gone completely, together with a couple of smaller dams, Germany's situation would have been really serious. This much was admitted by Reichsminister Speer under interrogation after the war, an occasion when, it is clear from his answers, he was concerned to flatter the United States' effort at the expense of the British.

What Speer did not emphasise were the long-term results of 617's bombing. Never again could any dam within the Reich be left with weak defences. Search-lights, guns, balloons, radar and highly trained personnel were pinned down on remote dam sites when they could have been better employed at the front. Guns unused were as good as guns destroyed – or, in other terms, the equivalent of munition factories bombed flat. The loss of life and property caused by Allied bombing have often been discussed. Less publicity has been given to the purely military effects. German figures released after the war show that in 1944 thirty per cent of all their artillery consisted of anti-aircraft guns, and that one-fifth of all guns heavier than 70mm were employed as Flak. Every 88mm used on air defence meant one less for the Panzers and anti-tank units. Similarly one-third of the German optical industry was employed on making gunsights etc for AA batteries, to the great detriment of army and navy, while one-half of the munitions sector of the electrical and electronic industries was engaged on radar work and signals. There was more to Gibson's great effort than dams.

The powers of darkness

Reichsmarshall Göring. He boasted 'No enemy plane will fly over the Reich territory'

The scene is Carinhall, Hermann Göring's country house headquarters near Berlin in 1943. Angry exchanges are taking place between the Reichsmarschall and Colonel-General Weise, in charge of anti-aircraft defences. 'How comes it, General, that relatively untrained crews in the RAF are able to find their way for hundreds of miles across Europe in the dark? Have Intelligence an answer to this question?'

The defence chief shuffles his feet, takes a deep breath and makes a statement. '*Jawohl, Excellenz!* Intelligence inform me that they do it by a combination of gravity, woodwind and a smell of bad eggs.' End of imaginary tableau. How else could a conscientious interpreter translate Gee, Oboe and H_2S?

There is no reason to believe, in fact, that the Germans learned the code-names for the RAF's various navigational and bombing aids before discovering the nature of the equipment itself: but had they done so a conversation on the above lines might really have taken place, with disastrous effects on the well-being of two very senior officers. Fortunately for Britain these navigational aids did exist and fortunately too Germany, although possessed of some very advanced electronic equipment, had not developed an exact equivalent of the British Chain Home coastal radar stations, able to measure both the heading and height of approaching

Anti-aircraft defence commander
Generaloberst **Hubert Weise**

raiders, and flash this to a central Control Room. Hitler had counted upon fighting an offensive war.

By the time Lancasters appeared on the scene Göring had had to eat his words about no enemy bomb falling on German soil, but the bombing, Whitehall had ruefully to confess, was of pretty random quality. One solution might have been tried, based on the Lorenz radio beams used by air lines before the war and by both air forces for blind approach techniques; but these had been used by the Luftwaffe in 1940. A pair of such beams, crossing above the target, accounted for the accurate bombing of Coventry; but the system was cracked by scientists at the Telecommunications Research Establishment (later renamed Radar Research Establishment), who found means of 'jamming' the beams in time to prevent Birmingham (and the Rolls-Royce works at Derby) from being 'Coventrated'. Radio beams

were not the answer. What navigators required was a universal means of route-finding in the dark; mere 'rat-runs' could be dangerous.

Also highly dangerous by the spring of 1942 were German searchlights, guns and night fighters. Casualties among bombers were running at four per cent, of which fighters took two-thirds and Flak one-third. A great deal had been learned during the months which followed the destruction of Rotterdam and Churchill's lifting of the ban on bombing German cities. The latter may not have suffered much but the defences were on the alert. In charge of night fighters, acting under Colonel-General Weise, Commander-in-Chief, home defences, was Major-General Kammhuber, a master of improvisation. His force originally consisted of two *Staffeln* or flights of twelve Messerschmitt 110 twin-engined two seater fighters (*Zerstörer*), a few of the new

twin-engined Ju 88 night fighters and a selection of Messerschmitt 109 single-seater day fighters. He also had one searchlight regiment and enough *Freya* early warning radar sets to form an experimental nucleus. *Freya* was a small fully mobile set with 360 degree coverage and a range of seventy-five miles, a good early warning set. Alongside it the Germans had a much higher-frequency set, the *Würzburg,* giving better definition, which was just what the searchlight batteries and AA gunners needed to engage their targets through cloud.

Bombers entering Germany by the most obvious route during the autumn of 1941 (along a front from the Danish border to Liège) found their presence announced by Freya early warning, and groups of searchlights ready and waiting for them near the target. In the centre of each group of four searchlights was a special blue-tinted 'master' beam, which shone vertically

Me 110s equipped with *Lichtenstein* radar for night-fighting

upwards until vectored on to a bomber by its Würzburg radar. Once the blue beam found an aircraft the other four lights held the victim in their cone and the master resumed the vertical, waiting for further custom. It was then up to the guns, and to night fighters, scrambled on receipt of radar warning, who had been waiting in orbit round radio beacons until the searchlights lit up their quarry.

This *Helle Nachtjagd* or illuminated night fighting was not the ideal. AA fire is as uncomfortable for night fighters as for bombers; neither guns nor fighters could get on with their job. Kammhuber moved his searchlights back from the towns and declared the searchlight belt out of bounds to all friendly aircraft not engaged in night fighting. He also divided his terrain into 'boxes' about

99

Above: Freya radar scanner on the French coast near Brest
Below: Ju 88 with the *Lichtenstein* equipment manufactured by Telefunken

twenty miles square, each the territory of a single night fighter. By August 1941 his line ran from the northernmost tip of Jutland to the Swiss frontier. Besides its fighter each box was equipped with a *Freya* and two *Würzburg* radar sets. The *Freya* 'found' and the *Würzburgs* worked as a couple – one striving to follow the bomber and the other tracking the fighter, while the movements of each were plotted by operators in the box's Control Room, which was in touch with the fighter by radio. When close enough the pilot could try his airborne radar. If that failed he could still sweep on into the searchlight belt for some *Helle Nachtjagd*.

By the start of the Lancaster era the Kammhuber line had grown in sophistication. The small mobile *Würzburg* had grown up into a static Giant *Würzburg* whose parabolic 'bowl fire' reflector measured twenty-five feet in diameter instead of ten, with an even narrower beam and a range of forty miles. *Freya*, too, had swollen into an immense structure (aptly named *Mammut*, 'Mammoth') standing thirty-five feet high and ninety feet wide. Its range was two hundred miles. The Telefunken company, makers of *Würzburg*, had also developed an excellent night fighter Airborne Interception radar, with a maximum range of two miles and a minimum range of two hundred yards, working on 490 megacycles.

The first four Ju 88 night fighters equipped with this set, *Lichtenstein*, became operational in February 1942. Pilots objected to the 'Christmas tree' of aerials sprouting from the aeroplane's nose – as pilots quite rightly always will – and preferred to rely on the now very effective ground-controlled system. But the Führer needed his searchlights elsewhere, and they were moved from the Kammhuber Line. Henceforth radar fighters were on their own. They quickly learned their job. Kammhuber's force expanded fast. By the time Lancasters began to figure in operations, and the

Above: The *Würzburg* radar
Below: The Giant *Würzburg* with a range of forty miles

Lancaster
18.10.43

Wellington
3.8.43

Halifax
30.7.43

Halifax 9.10.43

Short Stirling
26.7.43

Lancaster
22.9.43

Hali
27.9.

'Kill' markings on a *Würzburg* set
indicate at least three Lancasters

incendiary attacks on Rostock and the beautiful medieval town of Lübeck had shown the Führer that an area offensive had begun, there were four Wings *(Geschwader)* of night fighters; 265 machines, of which 140 could be serviceable any night. They were shooting down one bomber in twenty-five.

All the same, Germany lacked the flexibility in fighter control which had brought victory in the Battle of Britain and allowed Beaufighters to range far and wide during the night Blitz. Kammhuber's pilots were mewed up one to a box. This suited them very well so long as candidates entered the box one at a time, as they tended to do in the early days when each RAF navigator had only dead reckoning to find his way by. Formation flying, or even a fairly close stream through the boxes, if pilots could manage it, would completely upset the system.

The navigational aid which Bomber Command needed had existed since 1938, the invention of Mr R J Dippy. Service development followed rather slowly but by March 1942 – Lancaster time – enough sets existed to equip one-third of the bomber force. The device was code-named GEE, the initial letter of Grid, because it did in fact lay an invisible map-grid across Europe, based on the radar emissions of three ground stations in Britain laid out as an equilateral triangle with hundred-mile sides. 'It was all so simple', wrote Group Captain Dudley Saward, himself intimately concerned with radar development, in his book *The Bomber's Eye* (Cassell, London, 1959): 'Just switch on the receiver, adjust the controls and then read from the two calibrated lines across the face of the cathode ray tube the numbers indicated by the blips or deflections on the lines. Two readings were made on two different scales. Switch to the tenths and hundredths scale to obtain "B and C" readings, find these on the special lattice chart [a GEE Grid map of Europe], and your position was known'. GEE, nicknamed the Goon Box by aircrew and officially coded 'TR 1335' to lure the Germans into thinking it was a mere transmitter/receiver, became Bomber Command's magic map for the next

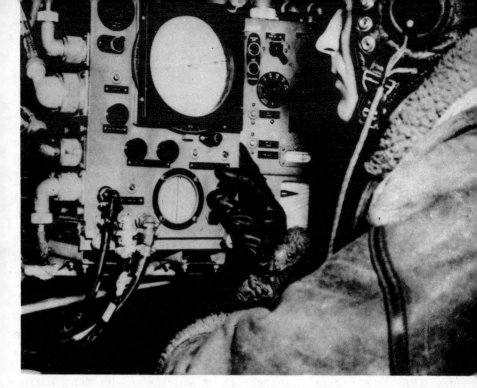

Left: With the addition of the new radar sets Ju 88 night fighters were able to shoot down one bomber in twenty-five. *Above:* GEE indicator unit and controls.
Below: The positioning of GEE and H₂S equipment in a Lancaster

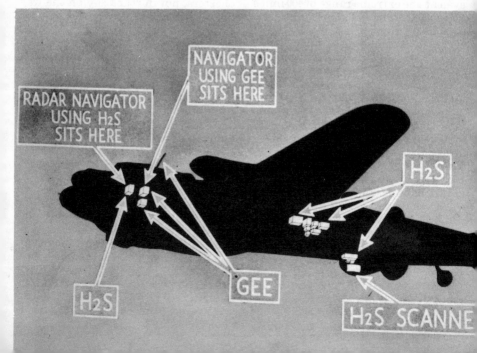

NAVIGATOR USING GEE SITS HERE

RADAR NAVIGATOR USING H₂S SITS HERE

H₂S

H₂S

GEE

H₂S SCANNE

five months, until the Germans found means to identify and jam its emissions. GEE was not accurate enough for bomb aiming, but it did permit navigators to find their position within six miles on the darkest night, even at the extreme range of 400 miles. More important still, it prevented the straggling which had been a feature of early bomber operations, and which played straight into Kammhuber's hands. The boxes were designed for a single fighter and a single customer at a time. Bombers flying on GEE were able to stay together. In this way they flew through each box in a stream, embarrassing the fighter with choice. They also arrived *en masse* at the target, overloading the defences there too. As a by-product, GEE remained a useful homing aid over Britain even when no longer of use over Germany, while the Lorenz beams (code-named J-beams) sent out by the RAF to distract attention from GEE also remained a valuable get-you-home service for any Bomber Command aircraft whose Goon Box was 'up the spout'.

The first use of a bomber stream took place on 30th May 1942 during Operation Millennium when, to dazzle the Americans and Russians, Harris put almost one thousand bombers into the air, including sixty-eight of the new Lancasters and thirty-five Manchesters, now fortunately on the way out. The period of attack was reduced from seven hours to two and a half, and losses fell slightly, to 3·8 per cent. Aircraft flew at different heights, forming what crews called a 'plate rack'. It was found that the risk of being bombed from above was better than the risk of being shot down by fighters. GEE remained un-jammed until 4th August 1942, when the Germans turned on speech transmitters to swamp the GEE pulses. This was a good run as things went in the 'radar war'.

Meanwhile Kammhuber built more boxes, as fighters and radar became more plentiful, placing them in tandem so that bombers were longer at risk. He was also equipping with the effective *Lichtenstein* night fighter radar. Bomber losses began to climb again.

However, jamming is a game that

two can play. TRE scientists realised that *Freya* early warning sets on the coast and similar sets inland used in conjunction with *Würzburg* could be dismayed by jamming, just as domestic television is upset by unscreened car ignitions. Precisely such a mischief-maker was produced and code-named Mandrel. It was small enough to be carried by the obsolete Boulton-Paul Defiant two-seater fighter; so nine Defiants were set to orbit at intervals along a two hundred mile stretch of enemy coastline, laying a screen of interference across two hundred miles' worth of German radar. Similar Mandrel transmitters were carried by two bombers in each main force squadron. Bombers could advance 'unseen'.

Not only electronic but also human aids to navigation were being introduced. Keen competition within Bomber Command to be 'top squadron' led naturally to the idea of special target-finding units like the Luftwaffe's Kampfgruppe 100, which had found and marked Coventry for the Main Force in November 1940. Controversy raged behind the scenes. Harris and

Merlin-engined Boulton Paul Defiant. These obsolete aircraft were fitted with Mandrel transmitters to create 'interference' on German radar screens

the AOC 5 Group, Air Vice Marshal the Hon Ralph Cochrane, were against the Pathfinder idea. It would create a *corps d'élite,* which was undesirable; the 'top squadron' idea was better. But they were overruled and Pathfinder Force was established in August 1942 under Group Captain DCT Bennett, Australian ex-airline pilot and navigator extraordinary, whom Harris later described as the most efficient airman he had ever met. Nonetheless Harris and Cochrane reserved the right to maintain a crack squadron of their own for very special jobs, for example, 106 (Lancasters) under Guy Gibson, which went after the German capital ships at Gdynia a few days after Pathfinder Force was announced, and Gibson's later command, the dambusting 617.

Pathfinder Force led off with a successful experimental raid on Emden. A few days later (30th August)

106 flew behind the Pathfinders as part of the main force. Gibson's description is worth quoting:

'A few days later we flew behind the Pathfinders to bomb Saarbrücken. We were carrying an 8,000-lb [High Capacity] bomb for the first time and great excitement prevailed on board as we waited in anticipation to see what they would do. Sure enough the Finders laid their long strings of flares, the Illuminators hovered around and then dumped bunch after bunch of flares right over the town; the bombs, incendiaries first, began to fall thick and fast, about 1,000 tons of them. Soon the whole area was one mass of flames . Everything was fine.

'But next day we heard very bad news from the photo-reconnaissance unit. The Pathfinder Force had boobed. They had lit up Saarlouis, a small town – in fact, a tiny town – ten miles from Saarbrücken . . .'

At this time, with GEE being jammed, Pathfinders had to depend upon dead reckoning, assisted by weather

Pathfinder markers show the way to the target

reports from reconnaissance Met Mosquitos.

Happily, accurate new aids to navigation and bombing were on their way, the 'woodwind' and 'bad eggs' which might so have disconcerted Göring's Intelligence men. The first of these was OBOE, so named because experimental sets had emitted a vaguely oboe-like note. This device, like the radar speed traps which motorists have learned to dread, depended upon the fact that radar 'echoes' from a body can be used to measure its range, and that accuracy does not decrease with range. The range itself was limited, since it was restricted by the curvature of the earth, and therefore OBOE equipment was installed at first in high-flying Mosquitos, whose altitude capability allowed them to operate usefully over the Ruhr. OBOE navigators were briefed to find their way closed to the target by GEE (which had been temporarily unjammed by Bomber Command technicians rather to the chagrin of the Ministry of Aircraft Production). They would then be picked up by a transmitting station at Dover whose OBOE pulses would be

transmitted back by the aircraft's own set giving the machine's exact distance from Dover. The radial distance to the target being known, the pilot was directed by radio to fly along the arc of a circle, centre Dover, which would pass through the target. A second ground station, at Cromer, would track it along this arc, and at the precise instant, bearing in mind altitude, bomb ballistics, winds and so on, release the bombs automatically. Provided the pilot was flying on a proper curve and not 'skidding' it was theoretically possible with OBOE to hit a target the size of Piccadilly Circus from 36,000 feet, even through thick fog. Later P F F Lancasters were occasionally fitted with OBOE, and it was while flying a Lancaster of 582 Squadron that Squadron Leader R A M Palmer, DFC and Bar, won a posthumous VC over Cologne two days before Christmas 1944. OBOE was limited by the fact that each pair of ground stations could handle only one aircraft at once, and each attack took between twelve minutes and a quarter of an hour. The ten minutes of steady flying along the approach arc were a highly nerve-racking time, needless to say. OBOE was first used on 20th December 1942.

Bomber Command's other device, whose name H_2S was a scientific pun by Lord Cherwell ('The Prof') on 'Home Sweet Home' and had nothing to do with sulphuretted hydrogen, at first went into service in Stirlings and Halifaxes, but shortly in Lancasters of 35 and 7 Squadrons, PFF as well. It was independent of ground stations. During experiments with airborne interception sets for night fighters it had been found that when the scanner was aimed not into space but at the ground, the quality of the 'echoes' received depended upon the nature of the terrain. Buildings and similar vertical surfaces returned a strong echo, showing as bright patches on the cathode-ray screen, while woodland showed up less brightly and flat surfaces such as fields or water appeared not at all. A rotary scanning aerial in the belly of an aircraft therefore could pick up a tolerable imitation of a map of the terrain below: hence the official name PPI – Plan Position Indicator. After a battle with Pathfinder Force, who asserted that H_2S was beyond the comprehension of Main Force crews, orders were issued on 21st February 1943 that all Lancasters should be fitted with it, except those carrying the 8,000-lb bomb, whose bomb-bay would have been fouled by the rotating scanner.

Rapidly the 'black boxes' increased, not only showing the way but protecting the bombers. An IFF (Identification Friend or Foe) device sorted returning bombers from enemy night intruders, provided it was still working of course. The identification of night fighters, too, came in for much attention, and a brace of not terribly popular detector sets came into use named 'Monica' and 'Boozer', the origin of many deplorable jokes. 'Monica' looked rearwards to detect aircraft up to 1,000 yards astern, uttering bleeps into the wireless operator's headphones which were usually caused by fellow-members of the bomber stream; 'Boozer' gave no such false alarms, but, being tuned to the emissions of every gun or searchlight laying *Würzburg* on the ground and every night fighter *Lichtenstein* in the sky, it continually cried 'Wolf!' and was consequently ignored.

It may be wondered why, when 'Mandrel' was so effective against *Freya* early warning sets, and the RAF had succeeded in jamming the Germans' night fighter R/T by the simple means ('Tinsel') of broadcasting the din from bombers' engines on a similar frequency until fighter pilot and controller could not hear each other speak, no steps had been taken towards the undoing of *Würzburg*, so effective for guns, searchlights and ground-controlled interception. The fact is that a perfectly good means of doing so existed, but Fighter Com-

mand would not allow it to be used, for the excellent reason that Germany had more bombers than Britain had, and that should her campaigns in Russia succeed a huge bomber force would be let loose on England. It was just possible that Germany had not thought of the device in question, so that it would be folly to present her with a weapon until we ourselves had discovered the antidote. Furthermore production of anti-*Würzburg* equipment took time.

The actual device was simple: *Würzburg*, operating on a higher frequency than *Freya*, was not sensitive to 'noise' jamming, but it could be readily misled. The ploy was to fill the air with interference by dropping strips of aluminium foil from aircraft, creating a myriad responses through which and behind which the bombers could sail along unscathed. The device was codenamed 'Window'. By July 1943 Britain had 'Window'-proof night

Left: 'Window' under manufacture.
Below: A Lancaster drops 'window' over Essen during one of the 1000 bomber raids

fighter and ground radar equipment and the tin foil strips, twelve inches long and three-eighths of an inch wide, backed with black paper and covered with lampblack on the metal side for invisibility to searchlights, were in full production. The ban was lifted as soon as the Allied landings in Sicily had been made, during which operation the Germans lost quantities of fighter aircraft – a fact which must have been rather heartening if it was made known to Bomber Command. Raiding Ruhr Valley and other frequent targets had become a costly business. Thanks to the *Würzburg* family of 53 centimetre (570 megacycles) radar, the Kammhuber Line had been doing well.

On 30th July 1943 the ban lifted and RAF bombers set forth en masse for Hamburg, navigating by H_2S to a target defined conspicuously by land and water and thus perfect for H_2S – and releasing clouds of 'Window'. Hence the firestorms of GOMORRAH. One phase of the radar war was over, and although bomber crews did not know it, a new phase of night fighting would shortly come in.

Gathering weight

Grand Slam is lowered onto its bomb train prior to bombing-up a Lancaster

During the nine months which culminated in the GOMORRAH attacks on Hamburg the Lancaster force had been gathering strength. The big Avro went first to 5 Group, which became an all-Lancaster unit. By September 1942 the Group mustered nine squadrons, numbers, 9, 44, 49, 50, 57, 61, 97, 106 and 207, all of which took part in the daylight low-level raid on Le Creusot on 17th October. This was a Main Force blow at the Schneider munitions works, plus a precision side-show operation by Gibson's 106 to 'take out' a generating and transformer station at Montchanin.

Next, the junior member of the Axis was attacked, with raids over the Alps against Turin and Milan and the port of Genoa, from which the Afrika Korps was provisioned. Thus the RAF backed up the army in time for the North African landings. Turin received its first 8,000-lb bomb; and amazingly during November 1942 5 Group flew 1,336 sorties over the Alps with the loss of only two aircraft, a record, Gibson pointed out, which any peacetime airline might be proud of. As the year drew to an end there were wide-ranging attacks on Germany: Duisburg in the Ruhr and even Munich. The addition of 467 Squadron (Royal Australian Air Force) brought 5 Group up to full strength, while 1 Group was also fast becoming an all-Lancaster unit. By February 1943 Wellingtons had been replaced by Lancasters in 12, 100, 101, 103 and 460 (RAAF) Squadrons. Already the Pathfinders, 8 Group, had

Packard Merlins on an American/Canadian Mk III Lancaster

The Avro Lancaster B III ME545 of No 218 (Gold Coast) Squadron flown by Flight-Lieutenant H F Warwick from Chedburgh in April/May 1945. The stripes on the fin indicate that the aircraft is part of a G-H squadron (Radar Blind Bombing System). The Lancaster III was the designation given to Lancasters otherwise identical to Mk Is but fitted with American Packard-built Merlins. Note the bulge under the fuselage containing the H2S (Airborne Radar Navigation and Target Location Device), which necessitated the removal of the ventral machine gun. *Engines:* Four Packard-built Merlin 28, 38 or 224. All other performance figures, armament, weights and dimensions as standard Mk I

two Lancaster squadrons, 83 and 156.

The Command now mustered 200 Lancasters, and it was an all-Lancaster force which raided Berlin on 16th January, doing little damage but stirring up fighters for the following night's sortie. Interceptors were getting dangerous: casualties were twenty-two lost and thirty-four damaged. This was the night on which Mark II Lancasters, with the air-cooled Bristol Hercules engines first went into action. Strategic (i.e. Admiralty) targets were also fashionable at this time, with attacks on naval dockyards and at U-boat pens at Saint-Nazaire, Lorient, Wilhelmshafen and La Spezia, as well as industrial targets – Hamburg and Milan during February. Then Harris opened his spring offensive, known in retrospect as the Battle of the Ruhr, starting with the first full-dress OBOE attack: 412 bombers, of which 140 were Lancasters, and another 22 Lancasters in Pathfinder Force. With OBOE it was possible to penetrate the industrial haze which had made the Ruhr such a chancy

target hitherto. During the battle, the first Mark III Lancaster, with Packard built Merlins, was delivered to 467 Squadron (April 1943). This machine was to be lost raiding Düsseldorff on the night of 11th-12th June. It was the first of more than 3,000 Mark IIIs. Meanwhile 3 Group had begun to go over to Mark IIs, the first full Hercules squadron being 115, which raided Berlin on 29th March.

The town of Friedrichshafen on Lake Constance has a dual place in Avro history. In August 1914 a trio of Royal Naval Air Service Avro 504 biplanes based in France bombed the Zeppelin sheds there and destroyed an airship; on 20th June 1943 a force of fifty-four Main Force Lancasters led by four Pathfinder Lancasters equipped with H_2S again bombed the factory, now making vitally important radar equipment for Luftwaffe night fighters. The raid destroyed or badly damaged one-half of the factory, and it is interesting for other reasons: the attacking force was controlled over VHF radio telephone by a master bomber in the style originated by Gibson on the Dams raid – a technique destined to be much used. German fighters left the attackers alone over the target despite bright moonlight, perhaps expecting to pick them off on the return journey. This time there was no return journey. Instead of turning west the Lancasters headed south, and crossed the Mediterranean to North Africa, where temporary servicing and re-arming depots had been established at Blida and Maison Blanche. Crews were able to enjoy a little sunshine before stocking up with wine, fruit and bombs, the latter for delivery in Italy during the homeward flight.

While Cochrane of 5 Group had reason to be pleased with the Friedrichshafen sortie, Harris's main concern was the Ruhr. During what Dr Noble Frankland, in *The Bombing Offensive against Germany, 1939-1945* (Faber and Faber London 1965), calls forty-three major actions between March and July, most of the steel, chemical, munitions and transport centres were bombed, by forces of 300 to 700 aircraft. This did not preclude attacks on more distant targets, such

as Nuremberg, Berlin (600 miles) and even Pilsen in Czechoslovakia, from which, on the second of two raids, 36 aircraft were lost out of 327, or nearly eleven per cent. Statistics for this Ruhr campaign give 18,406 as the number of sorties flown, from which 872 aircraft failed to return and a further 2,136 were damaged, a missing rate of some 4·7 per cent.

In the first engagement of 'the Battle of Hamburg', on 24th July, Lancasters predominated with 347 to 246 Halifaxes, 125 Stirlings and 73 Wellingtons. On the third visitation of GOMORRAH 329 Lancasters took part among the 740 bombers and dropped 1,426 tons of bombs. In the three raids a total of 8,621 tons of bombs, mostly incendiary, were dropped in addition to those delivered by the USAAF in daylight raids.

Meanwhile, even before the release of 'Window' German defences had improved. Because two-seater *Zerstörer* night fighters were slow to come through, an ex-bomber pilot named Hajo Herrmann suggested to General Weise, Kammhuber's superior, that a picked force of ex-bomber pilots

should be recruited to fly day fighters using the abundant light of fires, target indicators and searchlights. There were plenty of bomber pilots who were 'ex' at this time. Kammhuber believed strongly that Flak and fighters would not mix; to which Herrmann replied that Flak could be kept below a certain ceiling above which fighters could operate. Despite poor Flak liaison early experiments succeeded. On 3rd July a scratch force of seven Messerschmitt 109s and five FW 190s shot down twelve RAF bombers. Göring was enthusiastic. Major Herrmann was ordered to form a fighter wing of three FW 190 and Messerschmitt 109 single-seater squadrons. Thus was born the *Wilde Sau* (Wild Sow) tactic which was ready and waiting when 'Window' upset the earlier procedures.

By the third night's raid on Hamburg the fighters were really organised. The town was ringed with searchlights, and others were laid horizontally to show the path of the bombers. Herrmann's men, using the abundant light, flew until their fuel ran out, then landed for more. Towns put up 'lighthouses' of coloured flares to show fighters their way and soon fighters were ranging far and wide over Germany. Armed with toothbrush as well as cannon, pilots became independent of the home aerodrome, perhaps taking off from Denmark and fighting through to Bavaria. Out of the *fait accompli* there grew up a zonal system of control having more in common with Fighter Command than with Kammhuber's boxes. Often of course fighters were misled by 'Window' spoofs, decoy raids and changes of route. Without these, raiding distant targets would have been altogether

Right: US bombers follow the Lancasters in during the Battle of Hamburg
Left: Hitler's V-weapon establishment at Peenemunde after a raid by Lancasters. Seventeen were lost during this mission

too costly. As it was, the RAF lost seventeen Lancasters and twenty-three other heavies when 83 Squadron (Pathfinders) and 597 Main Force raided Peenemunde on the Baltic, Hitler's V-weapon establishment, on 17th August. Night fighters were misled until the operation was almost over; had they arrived sooner the carnage would have been terrific.

Accurate marking by the master bomber, Group Captain J H Searby made the raid a success and held back the rocket attack on London by several months: a good example of a 'panacea' raid. Lancasters were paying their way. After Peenemunde the Rhineland. Then Berlin on 23rd August. There was much to be said politically as well as strategically for raiding the capital; Londoners remembered the Blitz. However, the Luftwaffe could now hit back. Three raids during the last week in August cost Bomber Command 123 aircraft, partly because high-flying German bombers lit up the stream with flares dropped from above. On nights of thin cloud cover the defence played searchlight beams on the cloud base, forming

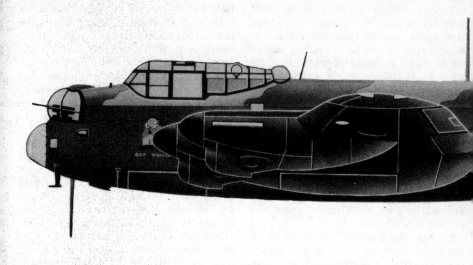

The Avro Lancaster I LL757 of No 101 Squadron, nicknamed 'Oor Wullie' and operating from Ludford Magna with Pilot-Officer R R Waughman as her pilot in May/June 1944. Note the two aerials protruding from the upper surface of the fuselage – an indication that LL757 was equipped with ABC 'Airborne Cigar', a device for misleading German fighter pilots. The device consisted of an operator in the fuselage who monitored the German fighter command radio channels and then broadcast misleading information and instructions on the same wavelength and in German to hinder fighter interceptions of bomber streams. Dimensions were Standard Mk I, but performance was a little lowered as a result of the extra weight and drag of the Airborne Cigar, while weights were slightly higher. Note also the original type of Manchester rear turret

a *Mattscheibe* or 'ground glass screen' against which the bombers showed in silhouette. Hermann's free-ranging banditti whose Wild Sow tactics had first been used on 20th April 1943 now benefited from new types of fighter: later Marks of Messerschmitt 110, improved Ju 88s and the new Heinkel 219. They also possessed some formidable radar equipment which allowed them to home on Mandrel jammers, H_2S transmissions and Monica, the fighter-warning device. Monica, treacherous hussy, was expelled, but during the late autumn and winter the practice of leaving H_2S switched

on was to cost BC many casualties, for German fighters learned to infiltrate the bomber stream on the way to the target and engage in long running fights, the so-called Tame Sow (*Zahme Sau*) tactics. It was not realised at the time, and is still not admitted in some quarters, that German monitoring stations could track the progress of a raid using H_2S all the way from home base to target.

Fortunately Wild Sow fighters depended largely on ground control, and VHF radio could be jammed. A powerful multi-waveband jammer named Airborne Cigar (ABC) was evolved and

carried in Lancasters of 101 Squadron, which mustered an extra operator as well as three formidable spar aerials, two on top of the fuselage and one under the chin. ABC Lancasters accompanied all raids from October 1943. German fighter pilots and controllers could no longer hear themselves speak, and when they turned on extra power, their chat was picked up in England, enabling the RAF to broadcast misleading information, fake met reports and general confusion on the controllers' wavelength. Hilarious three-cornered arguments took place between pilots, their ground-controller and German speaking RAF types, both chair-borne and airborne; and when the Germans switched to girl operators the RAF were ready with German-speaking Waafs. This kind of interference was called 'Corona'. A final and maddening form of Corona consisted of utterly boring and irrelevant test transmissions ('Testing, testing, testing, one, two, three, four, five. Testing ')warranted to jangle a fighter pilot's nerv-

es.Once the fighters made contact however, casualties were to be expected.

Among ordinary aircrew, of course, the subtleties of 'spoofing', jamming and the like were unknown. 'Sufficient unto the day . . .' Bad weather, with luck, might bring a night or two's respite, and there was always a gambler's interest in wondering what the next night's briefing would bring. It might be Happy Valley, or the Rhineland; on the other hand it might be a deep penetration job to Nuremburg or Munich or Leipzig, all of them on a 550-mile radius from Lincoln. Ample scope here for night fighters, Flak, searchlights and the other realities of a Lancaster pilot's life. For example, when night fighters spotted the head of the queue heading for Kassel they were able to shoot down forty-two of them (6·9 per cent) in compensation for much destruction in Kassel on 22nd October. Seventeen had been lost over Leipzig two nights before. Berlin, after the costly raids in August, had been left alone. At the end of the year Harris returned to the attack. 'We can wreck Berlin from end to end if the USAAF will come in on it', he told Churchill. 'It may cost us 400-500 air-craft. It will cost Germany the war.' The date of that minute was 3rd November 1943, a quite important date in Lancaster history. On that night G—H (a sort of 'OBOE' in reverse) was tried out in a Düsseldorff raid by 115 Squadron of 3 Group and 38 Mark II Lancasters of 6 (Canadian) Group.

There were technical reasons for using G—H on these machines rather than H_2S. Bristol Hercules engines gave 1,585hp at take-off, as against 1,280 from the Merlin 22, and so it was Bristol-engined Mark II Lancasters that were chosen to carry the 8,000-lb 'block buster' bomb which was too long to fit into a standard Mark I/III bomb bay. However, the long bomb bay of the Mark II left no room for the big H_2S rotary scanner, and G—H was fitted instead. This device was used experimentally on the Düsseldorff raid. Of the thirty-eight G—H Lan-casters fifteen attacked according to plan, sixteen had equipment failures

Allied bomber over Kassel

and went in with the main force, five returned early and two were posted missing. But, says Group Captain Dudley Saward, more than half the bombs dropped by G—H landed within half a mile of the aiming point, the Mannesmann steelworks. This was the raid in which Flight Lieutenant William Reid won the VC. Wounded in three places while still fifty minutes from target, he 'pressed on regardless', and continued to press on even when his wireless operator and navigator had both been killed or mortally wounded. Then he bombed the target and brought his Lancaster home.

A fortnight after Harris's historic signal a new series of Berlin raids began: the first of sixteen engagements known as the Third Battle of Berlin. The first took place on 18th November with the loss of only nine. For this raid the RAF had a new navigational device, H_2S Mark III working on a wave-length of 3cm instead of 10cm. Six special Lancasters were armed with this for Berlin and only one set broke down. H_2S Mark III worked well also for the raid of 22nd November, and on 3rd December it led Bomber Com-

mand to Leipzig, which was bombed despite heavy cloud. These sets emanated from TRE (Telecommunications Research Establishment), Malvern and were the work, it is interesting to discover, of Professor J B Lovell, now Sir Bernard, of Jodrell Bank. He was responsible also for 'Fishpond' a fighter warning instrument based on H_2S. Having invented the instrument in April 1943, Lovell had a model working within two weeks, a second model installed and flying within three. At the beginning of July Fishpond was on the bomber assembly lines being incorporated in the H_2S. Progress had not been 'through the usual channels'.

During November and December seven big raids were made on Berlin with surprisingly little loss. Winter weather did not encourage Wild Sow day-fighter ops. The Germans at this stage were baffled, with no antidote to H_2S, and Berlin, like Hamburg, was highly vulnerable to H_2S since a line of lakes pointed the way to the target and showed the shape of the city itself. They resorted to a ruse which both sides had used from time to time:

they built a full-scale model of Berlin fifteen miles away to the north-west made out of cardboard and plywood, with its own Flak and searchlight batteries, simulated bomb explosions, houses on fire – even a fake Tempelhof aerodrome. They also managed to confuse some of the opposition by throwing up imitation Pathfinder flares and markers. Sometimes during that winter the weather was so bad that even Cheshire, the new 617 CO, was unable to mark and some Pathfinders lost their way home.

The Lancaster was now undisputed 'Queen of the Heavies', having speed, ceiling and lifting-power that no other aircraft could match. This carried certain disadvantages. Lancasters could operate when others could not. It was an all-Lancaster force therefore, 680 strong, that went to Berlin on 14th January 1944, dropping 2,000 tons of bombs. On 20th January an even greater weight was dropped. Then came the disastrous Magdeburg raid of 21st January by Lancasters and Halifaxes, the first major defeat Bomber Command had suffered since the big raids on Berlin the previous

The Lancaster was by now the undisputed 'Queen of the Heavies'

summer. Magdeburg in Prussia, near Berlin, cost fifty-five Heavies out of 648 – 8·5 per cent. The Germans lost only seven night fighters.

So began a great rearguard action by the Luftwaffe, fought with as much gallantry and desperation as the Battle of Britain had been, with the difference that this battle took place in the dark.

A time had now come when Window no longer gave shelter from night fighter radar. The magic foil had jammed the Lichtenstein sets which had been the mainstay of the Kammhuber Line, but German scientists had now come up with an answer. Telefunken had rushed into production with a new set, SN-2, working on 90 megacycles, a frequency which normal Window would not jam. This was just the thing for Tame Sow fighting, and such was the fighting taking place over Berlin. Some very high scores were made, with Lancasters among the principal victims. At about 22.00 hours on 21st January 1944, during the Magdeburg raid, Sergeant Ostheimer, radar operator in a Ju 88 piloted by the most successful of current night fighter pilots, Major Prince zu Sayn-Wittgenstein, picked up a 'blip' on his AI screen. It was a Lancaster. The Prince opened fire, and flames came from the port wing of the Lancaster, which spun down and was seen to crash at about 22.05 hours. Bombers were so thick in the stream that Ostheimer picked up no fewer than six 'blips' at once. They made contact with a second Lancaster which received a short burst of cannon fire before diving away vertically on fire. Ostheimer felt heavy detonations as the Lancaster crashed – probably its bomb-load. This was between 22.10 and 22.15. Some ten minutes later the Junkers put a long burst of fire into yet a third Lancaster and watched it crash. Immediately afterwards

they picked out another four-engined bomber – probably a Halifax, and this too went down after only one firing pass.

This was close combat indeed; and the closeness of the in-fighting proved fatal to the Prince. After starting a small fire in a Lancaster which its crew managed to put out, the Junkers moved in for the kill; at the same moment this Lancaster or another in the stream opened fire and this time it was the Junkers that went down taking Sayn-Wittgenstein with it, although Ostheimer managed to bail out. The Prince's score was eighty-three 'kills', three more than that of Manfred von Richthofen, most successful fighter pilot in the First World War. Of the seven fighters shot down by bombers that night, another was flown by Captain Manfred Meurer, third highest scorer amongst the night fighter pilots. Adding his 65 to the Prince's 83, we have a total of 148. 'Tame Sow' and SN-2 were succeeding. With the latter set for 'seeing' and a device called Naxos-Z for homing on to H_2S, the fighter force was increasingly well equipped. Bomber Command lost 43 out of 683 over Berlin on 28th January and 42 out of 891 on 15th February. A Leipzig raid four days later was even more costly, with 78 casualties from a force of 823 – 9.5 per cent.

When the defences could be confused by diversionary flights – as they were on 20th–21st February – it was still sometimes possible to raid Germany without heavy loss. Only nine bombers were lost out of 598 and Stuttgart had a very bad time; but once the fighters caught hold it could be a bloody business. Three weeks later Stuttgart received 3,000 tons of bombs in one hour, but out of 863 bombers thirty-six did not come back. Over Berlin the climax came on 24th March; fighters were waiting, so that seventy-two bombers out of 811 were shot down, again a loss of almost 9 per cent. Even more disastrous was the last big deep-penetration flight of all, an expedition to Nuremberg on 30th March. Everything conspired against the bombers. Undeceived by Mosquito diversions the German controllers were able to funnel nearly 250 twin-engined Tame Sow night fighters into the stream before it was one-third of the way to the target. In a clear moonlit sky the bombers 'contrails' stood out conspicuously, and still further to brighten the scene a high-flying bomber squadron dropped parachute flares from above, lighting a beacon on which fighters from every quarter converged. Fortunately these did not include 'Wild Sow' squadrons; Bomber Command had successfully kept the enemy guessing as to the destination of the bombers, and so the single seaters stood off in case the target proved to be Frankfurt or Leipzig or Berlin.

The Kugelfischer ballbearing plant at Schweinfurt

Even so, with icing to add to their difficulties, the Command lost 96 heavies out of 795: a punitive 12 per cent, or in human terms 672 men killed or missing.

The brunt of all this fell upon Lancasters. During the attacks on Berlin representing 9,111 sorties, Lancasters made 7,256, or roughly 80 per cent, with 1,643 by Halifaxes, 162 by Mosquitos (mainly OBOE machines) and 50 by Short Stirlings, which now had neither the speed nor the ceiling for such operations. Losses had been dreadfully heavy. Between 18th November 1943 and the end of March 1944 thirty-five major raids cost 1,047 aircraft lost and 1,682 damaged. Had it not been for the remarkable strength of the Lancaster and its capacity to fly home with one or more engines 'u/s' casualties would have been higher still.

Besides the long-haul trips against

such targets as Stuttgart (aero-engines, vehicles), Schweinfurt (ball bearings), Augsburg (diesels, the Messerschmitt works), and Nuremberg (general and light engineering), there now came many short trips into Belgium and France. Lancasters were now helping to quench the railway system of Western Europe, especially junctions and sidings which would be needed by German armies rushing to repel any attack on *Festung Europa*. Small groups of Lancasters continued to slip out nightly for 'gardening', an inconspicuous and unsung job which Bomber Command crews kept up throughout the war. German ships moved into and out of harbour very much at their peril. It would be interesting to know how many tons of coastal shipping were lost purely through sea-mines laid by Roy Chadwick's design. Mine-laying was often no sinecure; there was always the

risk of being shot at by shore batteries, not to mention patrolling seaplanes and all the bad-weather hazards of night flying over a wintry North Sea. Fighters too were becoming a menace even on the short haul, with the introduction of Naxos and SN-2. After raiding Mailly-le-Camp in May – close to the champagne vineyards of NE France – Lancaster squadrons lost 42 out of 362 one night in early May. The Ruhr continued to receive a pasting, not always with very heavy loss, as witness an attack on Duisburg on 21st May, when 700 Lancasters dropped 2,000 tons of bombs, for 30 casualties, although even this represented 4.2 per cent.

D-Day was now quite close. Sealed orders for OVERLORD had gone out, special equipment was everywhere on site and personnel of every arm had been rehearsing special tricks, not least the Lancaster squadrons.

The tactical Lancaster

**With growing Allied mastery of the air
over Europe the Lancaster was
increasingly used for daylight bombing**

Ironically enough it was while the third Battle of Berlin was at its height and losses were mounting, that pressure was brought upon Harris to take part in a tactical war. For better or for worse, he was told, OVERLORD was brewing, and his bombers would be required to play their part. In vain he pleaded that heavy bombers were designed for strategic bombing at night, and that this was the way in which they should operate. Crews, he said, had no training in daylight, low-level operations, and aircraft had neither the armour nor the armament for such attacks. Furthermore any let-up on the bombing of industrial targets would give the enemy just the breathing space he needed. Harris was over ruled. This was really just as well because after the Berlin and Nuremberg raids it was Bomber Command which needed a respite and, as it turned out, the heavies proved far better at in-fighting than anyone had a right to expect.

The brief was that Harris should assist by bombing oil-supplies and what the American allies called 'transportation' targets. Bomber Command was not made part of the Allied Expeditionary Force, and characteristically the C-in-C managed to preserve a great deal of independence. 'Bert', his close friends predicted, would string along with the Air Staff and the Americans for as long as it suited him, and then get back to the main job, which was bombing Germany flat. They were remarkably right.

Tactical targets came upon the

Above: Crew and ground staff of Lancaster Y for Yoke of 153 Squadron, 5 Group, at Scampton, Lincolnshire 1944. *Right:* The marshalling yards at Tours after a raid. *Below:* Chewed and twisted trains and track after an RAF interdiction attack on the Trappes marshalling yards in Paris

agenda during the first week of March 1944 and soon crews became used to the short haul: trips to bomb marshalling yards in France, railways and canals in the Low Countries, factories and oil-plants.

Brilliant work was done by 617 Squadron under its new commander, Wing Commander Leonard Cheshire. They learned to dive-bomb with Lancasters, obtaining hitherto unheard of accuracy in bombing and marking. They removed an aircraft factory at Albert on 2nd March, and later that week took out a small but important needle-roller bearing works at St Etienne, without spilling bombs outside. On 18th March they blew up an explosives factory at Bergerac on the Dordogne and on the 19th a similar target at Angoulême. Both made a satisfactory bang. 'The powder works', radioed Cheshire, 'would seem to have outlived their usefulness.' On the way home from an abortive raid by 617 on Woippy, in Lorraine, Duffy's Lancaster was attacked by two Ju 88s and a FW 190. A bullet took his rear gunner, McLean, in the hand, but even so the latter shot down both Junkers, and possibly the Focke-Wulf too. Next night 617 were bidden to stop Michelins making tyres at Clermont Ferrand, but without damaging the works canteen or hurting French civilians. This they did with 12,000-pound bombs after low-level dummy runs. Another spot-marking feat by 617 during this time was an extreme-range attack on Munich, in which 200 Lancasters led by Cheshire's special marking Mosquito wrought extraordinary havoc.

As D-Day approached not only Lancasters but the other heavies, the day-bombers of 2 Group and, in huge measure, the US Army Air Forces, rained bombs on every conceivable target near the coast, being careful neither to concentrate on the actual invasion areas nor to build up into an obvious crescendo, either of which would have given the game away.

They were however careful to plaster coastal artillery and every discernible radar installation, while 5 Group made precision attacks also on railway yards at Rouen, Juvisy, near Paris, and the Gard du Nord itself. It was not always painless for the bombers. German night fighters now had Naxos AI equipment and could home on H_2S. They got 42 out of 362 Lancasters which had been bombing Mailly-le-Camp, not far from Rouen.

While the War Cabinet held its breath in case Hitler's unknown secret weapons should start up, and invasion hardware in the shape of landing-craft, flail tanks and Mulberry Harbour itself was mustering on the south coast, the greatest spoof of the war was in rehearsal.

Dr Robert Cockburn, Dr R V Jones, and others at the Malvern College headquarters of the Telecommunications Research Establishment had long been incubating a stupendous hoax. Using no ships at all they would create an impression on German coastal radar screens that two vast invasion fleets were crossing the Channel towards Boulogne and Fécamp, while the real invasion headed due south on to the Normandy beaches. 'Window' came into it of course - special six foot lengths of it, folded concertina-wise for easy

The radar jammer at Mont Couple near Calais enabled the German capital ships *Scharnhorst* and *Gneisenau* to make their unopposed Channel dash

handling, to fool German short-wave naval radar sets.

With helicopters the launching of this Window would have been easy, but no helicopters existed in those days. Instead, 617 Squadron's Lancasters and the Stirlings of 218 put on the most accurate display of night formation flying there has ever been, releasing Window so as to give the impression, as they advanced in overlapping orbits along a fourteen mile front in total darkness that a huge fleet was sailing towards France at a speed of eight knots. Cheshire's outfit navigated by GEE fixes, while the Stirlings used G-H, a sort of 'OBOE in reverse' developed by Dr E Frankland, in which the repeater was in the aircraft instead of on the ground.

While the two imaginary fleets, codenamed 'Glimmer' and 'Taxable' were under way and the actual invasion was crossing the Channel 101 Squadron's Lancasters plus a squadron of Flying Fortresses simulated a huge raid with Window up the Somme, with the object of attracting night fighters and jamming their VHF by means of no fewer than eighty-two Airborne Cigars. It may be mentioned while on this subject that one of the casualties caused by Bomber Command during the pre-OVERLORD sorties was the jammer at Mont Couple near Calais. This was the station which had blinded British coastal radar in 1942 while the battleships *Scharnhorst* and *Gneisenau* made their dash up Channel from Brest.

The RAF, sometimes blamed for not spotting the battleships despite darkness and bad weather – for German radar had never been mentioned, at least in public – now felt they had settled a score.

As the assault craft went in Lancasters were active over the beachheads. Heavy bombs on German coastal batteries so dazed the gunners that they could not shoot, whether the guns were knocked out or not, while behind, accurate bombing of roads, railways and bridges around

A 'Tallboy' due for delivery against the E-boat pens at Le Havre. An extended bomb-bay was necessary for this weapon

Caen and Vire greatly hindered enemy reinforcements. Then there was the Saumur Tunnel.

If 617 had felt frustration at orbiting over the Channel while others were in a shooting war, they now had their chance, and their weapon. A tunnel running deep through a hill was precisely the sort of thing for which Dr Barnes Wallis had designed his earthquake bombs. Grand Slam had not yet been made, but Tallboy was in production although scarce. The tunnel lay on the main line running south to Bordeaux through which German armour was expected to come. Navigating by H_2S, four Lancasters of 83 Squadron marked the target with sticks of flares and Cheshire's types in

eighteen Lancasters went through their Annie Oakley routine. McCarthy, from Brooklyn, scored a direct hit on a marker. One bomb sliced through the hill to burst on the permanent way. The tunnel was blocked and Tallboy proven. Next the big bomb was taken by 617 to Le Havre, for use against E-boat pens. The pens were wrecked and 113 E-boats – Germany's fast anti-shipping gun boats – were lifted from the water by the ensuing tidal wave. 'If the Navy had done that', muttered Harris, 'it would have counted as a great sea victory.'

Bomb damage in Le Havre after an RAF mission

Lancasters now operated in daylight for the first time since 1942. At last they had the luxury of fighter escorts and targets were relatively close at hand. Lancasters made big day and night attacks on Boulogne and Le Havre E-boat pens the day of Cheshire's Tallboy raid; but there were 'strategic' raids as well, to destroy Hitler's synthetic oil plants, and casualties were very heavy. Wesseling, close to Cologne, especially was no 'piece of cake'. On the longest night of 1944 three squadrons (619, 44 and 49) each lost six out of sixteen Lancasters and from East Kirby base another seventeen crews failed to return. Another somewhat lethal activity was low-level bombing at night in support of the army. This demanded great accuracy, but it was also exhilarating, and provided a welcome opportunity for Lancaster gunners to shoot back. The wheel had come full circle. Once upon a time German day bombers and ground support aircraft had bombed London at night; now British night bombers were supporting the army night and day.

V stands for *Vergeltung*, which means reprisal. Conveniently forgetting that it was he who started area bombing, Hitler chose this name for his robot weapons – the V1 flying bomb, the V2 rocket and V3, an immense subterraneous gun with 500 foot barrel aimed at London. The outward and visible sign of these weapons

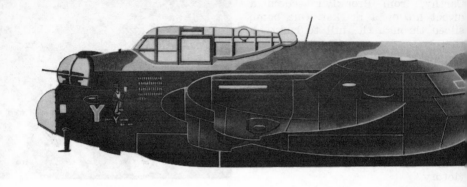

P-51 North American Mustang

The Avro Lancaster B I LM220 of No 9 Squadron flown by Flight-Lieutenant W D Tweddle from Bardney in November 1944. This was one of three Lancasters of No 9 Squadron to be modified to carry the 12,000lbs 'Tallboy' bomb, so that they could operate with the other modified Lancasters of No 617 Squadron against the *Tirpitz* in Norway. To give a better range and performance, Merlin 24s were fitted and the mid-upper turret eliminated. To accommodate the bomb, special bulged bomb bay doors were fitted. An extra fuel tank was fitted in the fuselage to give extra range

took the form of concrete emplacements and tunnels, barely to be seen from the air. Missiles started falling on London as invasion troops came ashore. The counter-weapon for these was Tallboy, capable of penetrating a vast thickness of concrete by direct hit, or seismically undermining foundations when placed alongside. The technique was for Leonard Cheshire to mark in daylight with smoke bombs from his Mosquito – later changed for a North American P-51 Mustang – going down to 500 feet. Then 617's Lancasters would launch their Tallboys by the new Stabilised Automatic Bomb Sight (SABS) from 18,000 feet. In this way they took out the ski-sites one by one, blew up an underground rocket store at Siracourt and the V3 installation at Mimoyecques. Ironically Hitler's scatter-weapons had been beaten by the most accurate bombing ever achieved; his U-boat pens, also small and heavily concreted, collapsed under the same assault.

Main force Lancasters meanwhile bombed German garrisons holding out at Caen and elsewhere, raided German airfields in Holland and struck at tactical targets as requested by the army. Mark II Lancasters from 3 Group became renowned for their daylight bombing, and later the group urged Harris to allow them some daylight raids on Germany, dropping 8,000 pounders and navigating by G–H. Low-level bombing in daylight was often a desperate business, as pilots held their machines on course through curtains of Flak and the tracer shells – aptly named *Leichenfinger* by the Germans, 'Dead Men's Fingers' – rose to grope them out of the sky. All in all, though, the OVERLORD operations proved a respite for Bomber Command. Casualty figures speak for themselves. From 5 per cent in February they sank to 3 per cent in March, 2 in April, less than 3 in May, 2 in June, 2 in July, 1·2 in August and 2 in September.

As General Eisenhower's armies bogged down after an exceptionally wet August Bomber Command turned once more from tactical to strategic targets.

Paravane
and beyond

German battleship *Tirpitz* at anchor in
Alten Fjord

Most certainly 'strategic' in A M Harris's sense of the word was Operation PARAVANE. The Admiralty were highly concerned about the presence of the battleship *Tirpitz* at Alten Fjord in Norway. If once she got out into the Atlantic or North Sea no shipping convoy would be safe. *Tirpitz* was sister ship to the *Bismarck*, 45,000 tons of guns and armour plate, with two horizontal layers, 2 inches and 3·2 inches thick. Propaganda proclaimed her unsinkable. Attempts had already been made by Bomber Command and the Fleet Air Arm to the tune of 754 sorties with the loss of 32 aircraft. The Russians too had had a go. So had midget submarines and Fairey Barracuda torpedo carriers. *Tirpitz* had been damaged enough to keep her in dock, but the threat remained.

Tallboy seemed a possible answer, but at Alten Fjord she was just beyond Tallboy range. Arrangements were made for 617 under its new commander, Wing Commander J B Tait, DSO DFC, (Cheshire having been given a rest and the VC) to operate from Russia, together with seventeen other 5 Group Lancasters from 9 Squadron. On a first expedition, leaving England for Yagodnik, near Archangel, on 11th September, seventeen Tallboys were dropped. *Tirpitz*, reported a PRU Mosquito, was bloody but reasonably unbowed: nine months' worth of

Fairey Barracudas off the coast of Norway

Above: *Tirpitz* after at least two direct hits from 617 Squadron's 'Tallboys'
Below: B-17 Flying Fortresses of the Eighth USAAF over Berlin

damage. She was now moved to Haak Island, near Tromsö, just, but only just, within reach from Scotland. With extra tankage to bring the fuel load to 2,406 gallons the Lancasters could make it. And if fitted with Merlin 24s they could lift this load and their Tallboys into the air, as the 24 gave an extra 340hp each for take-off – 1,620hp at 3,000 revs.

On 12th November thirty-eight Lancasters left Lossiemouth at three in the morning and arrived over the *Tirpitz* at 9am. They all carried Tallboys, in contrast with the earlier raid when some 'Johnnie Walker' bombs had been unsuccessfully tried. These were a sort of subaqueous yo-yo supposed to bob up and down in the water and explode against the ship's bottom.

Perhaps the daring of a daylight attack took the defences by surprise. There was no smoke screen, no fighters went up and the sky was clear. Twenty-eight Tallboys were dropped and there were at least two direct hits. The *Tirpitz* turned turtle, immuring most of her ship's company, and sank in shallow water, most probably a victim, also, of the Stabilised Automatic Bomb Sight used by 617. They bombed from 14,000 feet, which for the record is a range of a little over two and a half miles.

During the time that 617 were learning to use Tallboy they were awaiting, although they did not know it, an even bigger bomb. Pathfinder and Main Force squadrons, supported by the electronic wizardry now concentrated in 100 Group under Air Commodore Addison with 200 aircraft, were free to fly where they wished. With its day fighters largely shot down in combating the Flying Fortress armadas of the Eighth USAAF and its night fighters increasingly bedevilled by British AI, the Luftwaffe gave little opposition. Despite strong political and Staff pressure to narrow his attacks on to specific targets such as oil refineries and ball-bearing works, Harris re-embarked on an era of mass destruction. He believed that if all the yellow pages could be ripped from the directory, industry, commerce and the social life of a country must come to an end. During the last three months of 1944, says the record, 163,000 tons of bombs were dropped, of which the two-ton (4,000-lb) blockbusters habitually carried by Lancasters (and by no other heavy aircraft, British or American) made up a large proportion. By August 1944 Bomber Command had over 1,000 aircraft in front line service, and the heavies were bombing by day as well as by night. Six months later, in April 1945, the Command was almost half as large again and Lancasters alone amounted to 1,087, supported by 34 Halifaxes and 170 Mosquitos.

There is unfortunately no room here to explore the various techniques for marking used by Pathfinder Force on the one hand and by 5 Group on the other. Both had great success, and as the short-range war developed new 'precision' targets came on the agenda. During November and December synthetic oil plants at Castrop, Leuna and Politz were raided with dire effect on Luftwaffe fuel supplies, while as the New Year came in 5 Group despatched nine squadrons to let the water out of the Dortmund-Ems canal, whose importance in delivering Ruhr-made munitions was even greater now that so many railways lay in ruins. The point chosen was Ladbergen, where aquaducts made it especially vulnerable. A number of Lancasters were lost or damaged, including the 9 Squadron machine in which Flight Sergeant Thompson won the Victoria Cross. The canal was emptied over an important stretch, many loaded barges being left high and dry.

Meanwhile for targets beyond immediate persuasion Dr Barnes Wallis's biggest missile was incubating: the ten-ton (actually 22,000 pound) 'earthquake' bomb made from special armour-piercing steel and known as Grand Slam. This was the design upon which Tallboy had been based. Now targets lay within range to which the monster

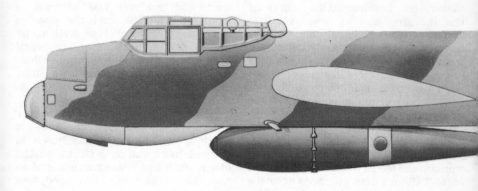

The Avro Lancaster B I (Special) PD133 of No 617 Squadron operating from Woodhall Spa in 1945. The B I (Special) was a modification to enable single stores of over 12,000lbs weight to be carried. Illustrated is a B I (Special) of the 'Dambusters' squadron carrying the largest bomb to be used in the war, the Barnes Wallis-designed 22,000-lb 'Grand Slam'. This was a bomb intended to be dropped from a considerable height so that it should be supersonic by the time it hit the ground. It would then penetrate some 400 feet into the ground before exploding and setting up an earthquake-like shock wave, which would shake down any structure in the near vicinity. The weapon was used for the first time, with complete success, against the Bielefeld Viaduct on 13th March, 1945. Both the nose and mid-upper turrets were removed and plated over to save weight and drag, and a new type of undercarriage, developed for the Lancaster's successor, the Lincoln, was fitted to take the considerable extra weight of the bomb. Specifications were as standard B I except in the following instances. *Armament:* Two .5-inch Browning machine guns in Frazer-Nash 82 rear turret and one 22,000-lb bomb. *Speed:* 200mph at 15,000 feet. *Range:* 1,550 miles. *Weight empty/loaded:* 35,457/72,000lbs

could be delivered – by Lancasters specially modified for 617. Their first target came on 14th March 1945, the Bielefeld viaduct carrying the main line from Hamm to Hanover which had already survived Tallboy and US Eighth Army Air Force attacks. An earthquake cavern below and to one side effectually brought down a hundred-yards stretch. The Arnsberg viaduct, another Ruhr approach bridge, fell to Grand Slam a few days later; then the Arbergen bridge near Bremen, where Tallboys scored two direct hits and 217 lost an aircraft. On 23rd March three out of four Lancasters scored direct hits on yet another

munitions-delivery bridge, at Nienburg, near Bremen.

As a change from bridges they went after a battleship again, when news came that Germany's third and last pocket battleship the *Luetzow*, was lying at Swinemunde on the Baltic, a high-level target for the SABS. Twice 617 drove all across Europe in vain. Cloud hid the target each time. On the third trip, with fighters and Flak fully alert, almost every one of the eighteen Lancasters was holed by shrapnel or cannon fire, despite an escort of Mustang long-range fighters; one was lost to a direct hit from Flak and two others turned home on three engines.

The North American Mustang and its drop tanks – called by contemporary pressmen 'jettisonable' – made daylight operations feasible. Oddly, the need for an escort fighter seems to have been overlooked by successive Staff and Ministry planners, just as the need for heavy bombers had been overlooked by the Germans.

During the last few months of hostilities when factories lay flat and fuel either did not exist or was untransportable, the German aircraft industry miraculously brought new types into service: the Messerschmitt 410 twin-

The ten-ton earthquake bomb 'Grand Slam'. This was first used on the Bielefeld viaduct raid in March 1945

engined fighter, the Me 262 twin-engined jet fighter (the first jet in operational service with any air force) and, most fantastic of all, the Me 163B rocket-propelled interceptor. This could climb to 30,500 feet in 2·6 minutes but had a duration of only 7½ minutes under power.

When the 163B's motor had used up its fuel, consisting of hydrogen peroxide and petrol, the pilot was faced with a perilous glide back to earth followed by a 140mph landing on a central skid, without either wheels or brakes, the undercarriage having been jettisoned after take-off. These were brought in primarily as an anti-Mosquito weapon. Mosquitos had acquired much the same bogey-man status as Fokker E IIIs had enjoyed

during 1915. To deal with them late Marks of Ju 88 were fitted with nitrous-oxide injection, which made them 25mph faster than the British 'wooden wonder'.

In the spring of 1945 therefore the Luftwaffe's fighter squadrons came briefly to life again. Using Naxos and SN-2 they staged intruder operations over East Anglia in the early hours of 4th March. Coming in low from the North Sea below radar cover, and homing on the bombers' H$_2$S, they shot machines down as they were landing, or en route for home with station-keeping lights switched on. At this time there were more than one hundred bomber bases in East Anglia not counting those of the US Air Forces. Although fuel shortage seri-

ously limited Luftwaffe flying, and improved types of Window, spoofing and jamming kept many fighters at bay, intruder pilots managed to pile up formidable scores. The highest of these belonged to Major Heinz-Wolfgang Schnaufer, who finished the war with 123 confirmed, including nine heavy bombers in a day. Even at this stage in the war bombing could be a 'dicey business'. For example: on 16th March a force of 231 Lancasters from 1 Group and 46 Pathfinders, intercepted during raids on Würzburg and Nuremberg, lost twenty-four, a casualty rate of nearly 9 per cent – most unusual at

Me 262, the first jet in operation during the war but soon relegated to an impracticable bombing role by Hitler

Above: Sacks of food are loaded aboard a Lancaster prior to Operation *Manna* over Holland. *Below:* A Lancaster is 'bombed-up' with a bouquet of red roses, carnations and lilac for delivery to Queen Wilhelmina on the first anniversary of Operation *Manna*

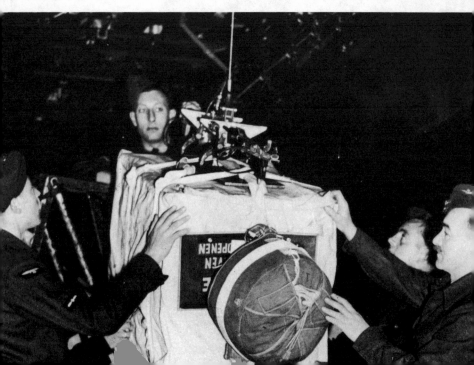

this stage. Mainly however during the last months of the war radar by night and Mustang escorts by day kept the bomber force fairly safe.

Such an escort went with 617 to Berchtesgaden on 25th April when the Dam Busters, fresh from grand-slamming the Luetzow at Swinemunde, hoped to find Hitler at home. The Führer was in fact in Berlin, and cloud shrouded the Eagle's Nest; it mattered little. He was to die five days later with Eva Braun in the shelter beneath the Chancellery. The bombs demolished a near-by SS barracks.

Next night came the last Lancaster raid of the war, when 119 machines from 5 Group raided U-boat fuel storage tanks at Vallo in Oslo Fjord. The master bomber on that occasion was Wing Commander Maurice A Smith, DFC and Bar, later Editor of *Flight International*.

When, some ten years later, the Lancaster was at last pensioned off by the RAF he had this to say in a *Flight*, article, 'Lancs at War':

'I do not remember ever having met a pilot who did not like the Lanc. Most men in Bomber Command had a profound confidence in the ability of the aircraft and its four Merlins to get them home, come what might ...

'Perhaps considerably discouraged by his inability to land a Stirling as it ought to be done, a new-from-Conversion-Unit pilot was taken off for a circuit or two in a dual Lancaster and then launched with his crew ... Except for the fairly limited space, he liked almost everything around him better than any previous bomber of his experience. Here was a machine with response and spirit, which reacted to its controls like a big Tiger Moth. It enjoyed bags of bank, and it three-pointed instinctively. You could see out of it well; it would fly on any two engines, there was power to spare; the brakes worked well.

'Lancs were kind to their crews. They helped to keep calm in really rough weather . . . They could call upon remarkable reserves of power and strength. There was the 44 Squadron machine that was blown on to its back by a near miss and eventually pulled out of the dive almost at ground level. Dozens of under-wing rivets had torn out; and the dihedral, visible even in the early light next morning, would have suited an elastic-driven model.

'There was another fully-loaded machine that was spun over Stuttgart at 20,500 feet and recovered in time to make another run, and drop its bombs at 18,000 feet. Seeing 'activity' lower down, one machine came home happily at 26,000 feet – a good altitude for a wartime bomber ...

'The most remarkable performance of all was the lifting of the first 12,000 pound, then 22,000 pound bombs. The aircraft were operational at Woodhall Spa and took off at an all-up weight of well over twice their empty weight. Nose and mid-upper turrets had been removed, and Rolls-Royce had found some more boost, but they were still operational Lancs with crew, extra equipment for the bomb and tail armament.'

Built in more than 7,000 examples, the Lancaster had indeed come a long way from the four-engined 'Manchester III' prototype whose first flight, watched with crossed fingers by Avro 'top brass' had been made in January 1941. In no time at all this machine, re-named Lancaster, swiftly and completely lived down its twin-engined Manchester origins to become during four and a quarter years of war one of the most successful machines the RAF ever had, far exceeding all other Heavies in fame and popularity. The two Roys, Chadwick and Dobson, each in his own way was proud of the Lancaster, and countless aircrew had reason to be grateful for its strength.

A few days after the Berchtesgaden and Oslo raids Lancasters of the RAF embarked upon their first peacetime operation, a life-saving sortie this time, known to history as Operation *Manna*, which consisted of dropping food parcels to the starving Dutch.

The Lancaster VCs

Ten Victoria Crosses were awarded to Lancaster aircrew. How many more were deserved it is impossible to say. There must have been untold acts of heroism and self-sacrifice in the aircraft which failed to return.

The following extracts from *The London Gazette* are reprinted as a tribute, and because they set down, in stark official language, some of the varied and appalling hazards which must have beset every crew more than once on every operational tour of thirty sorties.

Acting Squadron Leader John Dering Nettleton VC

Acting Squadron Leader John Dering Nettleton (41452), No 44 (Rhodesia) Squadron.

Squadron Leader Nettleton was the leader of one of two formations of six Lancaster heavy bombers detailed to deliver a low-level attack in daylight on the diesel engine factory at Augsburg in Southern Germany on 17th April 1942. The enterprise was daring, the target of high military importance. To reach it and get back, some 1,000 miles had to be flown over hostile territory.

Soon after crossing into enemy territory his formation was engaged by 25 to 30 fighters. A running fight ensued. His rear guns went out of action. One by one the aircraft of his formation were shot down until in the end only his own and one other remained. The fighters were shaken off but the target was still far distant. There was formidable resistance to be faced.

With great spirit and almost defenceless, he held his two remaining aircraft on their perilous course and after a long and arduous flight, mostly at only 50 feet above the ground, he brought them to Augsburg. Here anti-aircraft fire of great intensity and accuracy was encountered. The two aircraft came low over the roof tops. Though fired at from point blank range, they stayed the course to drop their bombs true on the target. The

second aircraft, hit by Flak, burst into flames and crash-landed. The leading aircraft, though riddled with holes, flew safely back to base, the only one of six to return.

Squadron Leader Nettleton, who has successfully undertaken many other hazardous operations, displayed unflinching determination as well as leadership and valour of the highest order.

Personal note: John Nettleton was a South African born in Natal and educated in Cape Town. He spent 18 months at sea in the merchant service before coming to England to join the Royal Air Force in 1938. He trained as a pilot and was promoted Squadron Leader when only 24 years old. He was killed in action later in the war.

Wing Commander Geoffrey Leonard Cheshire, DSO DFC (72021), Royal Air Force Volunteer Reserve, 617 Squadron.

This officer began his operational career in June 1940. Against strongly-defended targets he soon displayed the courage and determination of an exceptional leader. He was always ready to accept extra risks to ensure success. Defying the formidable Ruhr defences, he frequently released his bombs from below 2,000 feet. Over Cologne in November 1940, a shell burst inside his aircraft, blowing out one side and starting a fire; undeterred, he went on to bomb his target. About this time, he carried out a number of convoy patrols in addition to his bombing missions.

At the end of the first tour of operational duty in January 1944, he immediately volunteered for a second. Again, he pressed home his attacks with the utmost gallantry. Berlin, Bremen, Cologne, Duisberg, Essen and Kiel were among the heavily-defended targets which he attacked.

He started a third operational tour in August 1942 when he was given command of a squadron. He led the squadron with outstanding skill on a number of missions before being appointed in March 1943 as a station commander.

In October 1943 he undertook a fourth operational tour, relinquishing the rank of group captain at his own request so that he could again take part in operations. He immediately set to work as the pioneer of a new method of marking enemy targets involving very low flying. In June 1944 when marking a target in the harbour at Le Havre in broad daylight and without cloud cover, he dived well below the range of the light batteries before releasing his marker-bombs, and he came very near to being destroyed by the strong barrage which concentrated on him.

During his fourth tour which ended in July 1944, Wing Commander Cheshire led his squadron personally on every occasion, always undertaking the most dangerous and difficult task of marking the target alone from a low level in the face of strong defences.

Wing Commander Cheshire's cold and calculated acceptance of risks is exemplified by his conduct in an attack on Munich in April 1944. This was an experimental attack to test out the new method of target marking at low level against a heavily defended target situated deep in Reich territory. Munich was selected, at Wing Commander Cheshire's request, because of the formidable nature of its light anti-aircraft and searchlight defences. He was obliged to follow, in bad weather, a direct route which took him over the defences of Augsburg and thereafter he was continuously under fire. As he reached the target, flares were being released by our high-flying aircraft. He was illuminated from above and below. All guns within range opened fire on him. Diving to 700 feet, he dropped his markers with great precision and began to climb away. So blinding were the searchlights that he almost lost control. He then flew over the city at 1,000 feet to assess the accuracy of his work and direct other aircraft. His own was badly hit by shell fragments but he

Wing Commander Geoffrey Leonard Cheshire VC, DSO, DFC

continued to fly over the target area until he was satisfied that he had done all in his power to ensure success. Eventually, when he set course for base, the task of disengaging himself from the defence proved even more hazardous than the approach. For a full twelve minutes after leaving the target area he was under withering fire but he came safely through.

Wing Commander Cheshire has now completed a total of 100 missions. In four years of fighting against the bitterest opposition he has maintained a record of outstanding personal achievement, placing himself invariably in the forefront of the battle. What he did in the Munich operation was typical of the careful planning, brilliant execution and contempt for danger which has established for Wing Commander Cheshire a reputation second to none in Bomber Command.

Wing Commander Cheshire was one of the most decorated men in the RAF, having won the DSO in December 1940, DFC in March 1941, and Bar to the DSO in April, 1941. Twelve months later he added another Bar to his DSO.

He was born in 1917 at Chester and was educated at Stowe and Merton College, Oxford, where he was a member of the University Air Squadron between 1937 and the outbreak of war.

Acting Flight Lieutenant William Reid VC

Acting Flight Lieutenant William Reid, RAFVR, No 61 Squadron.

On the night of November 3rd 1943, Flight Lieutenant Reid was pilot and captain of a Lancaster aircraft detailed to attack Düsseldorf.

Shortly after crossing the Dutch coast, the pilot's windscreen was shattered by fire from a Messerschmitt 110. Owing to a failure in the heating circuit, the rear gunner's hands were too cold for him to open fire immediately or to operate his microphone and so give warning of danger; but after a brief delay he managed to return the Messerschmitt's fire and it was driven off.

During the fight with the Messerschmitt, Flight Lieutenant Reid was wounded in the head, shoulders and hands. The elevator trimming tabs of the aircraft were damaged and it became difficult to control. The rear turret, too, was badly damaged and the communications system and compasses were put out of action. Flight Lieutenant Reid ascertained that his crew were unscathed and, saying nothing about his own injuries, he continued his mission.

Soon afterwards, the Lancaster was attacked by a Focke Wulf 190. This time, the enemy's fire raked the
152

bomber from stem to stern. The rear gunner replied with his only serviceable gun but the state of his turret made accurate aiming impossible. The navigator was killed and the wireless operator fatally injured. The mid-upper turret was hit and the oxygen system put out of action. Flight Lieutenant Reid was again wounded and the flight engineer, though hit in the forearm, supplied him with oxygen from a portable supply.

Flight Lieutenant Reid refused to be turned from his objective and Düsseldorf was reached some 50 minutes later. He had memorised his course to the target and continued in such a normal manner that the bomb aimer, who was cut off by the failure of the communications system, knew nothing of his captain's injuries or of the casualties to his comrades. Photographs show that, when the bombs were released, the aircraft was right over the centre of the target.

Steering by the Pole star and the moon, Flight Lieutenant Reid then set course for home. He was growing weak from loss of blood. The emergency oxygen supply had given out. With the windscreen shattered, the cold was intense. He lapsed into semi-consciousness. The flight engineer, with some help from the bomb aimer, kept the Lancaster in the air despite heavy anti-aircraft fire over the Dutch coast.

The North Sea crossing was accomplished. An airfield was sighted. The captain revived, resumed control and made ready to land. Ground mist partially obscured the runway lights. The captain was also much bothered by blood from his head wound getting into his eyes. But he made a safe landing although one leg of the damaged undercarriage collapsed when the load came on.

Wounded in two attacks, without oxygen, suffering severely from cold, his navigator dead, his wireless operator fatally wounded, his aircraft crippled and defenceless, Flight Lieutenant Reid showed superb courage and leadership in penetrating a further 200 miles into enemy territory to attack one of the most strongly defended targets in Germany, every additional mile increasing the hazards of the long and perilous journey home. His tenacity and devotion to duty were beyond praise.

Pilot Officer Andrew Charles Mynarski (CAN/J87544) (Deceased), Royal Canadian Air Force, No 419 (RCAF) Squadron.

Pilot Officer Mynarski was the mid-upper gunner of a Lancaster aircraft, detailed to attack a target at Cambrai in France, on the night of 12th June 1944. The aircraft was attacked from below and astern by an enemy fighter and ultimately came down in flames.

As an immediate result of the attack, both port engines failed. Fire broke out between the mid-upper turret and the rear turret, as well as in the port wing. The flames soon became fierce and the captain ordered the crew to abandon the aircraft.

Pilot Officer Mynarski left his turret and went towards the escape hatch. He then saw that the rear gunner was still in his turret and apparently unable to leave it. The turret was, in fact, immovable, since the hydraulic gear had been put out of action when the port engines failed, and the manual gear had been broken by the gunner in his attempt to escape.

Without hesitation, Pilot Officer Mynarski made his way through the flames in an endeavour to reach the rear turret and release the gunner. Whilst so doing his parachute and his clothing, up to the waist, were set on fire. All his efforts to move the turret and free the gunner were in vain. Eventually the rear gunner clearly indicated to him that there was nothing more he could do and that he should try to save his own life. Pilot Officer Mynarski reluctantly went back through the flames to the escape hatch. There, as a last gesture to the trapped gunner, he turned towards him, stood to attention in flaming

Pilot Officer Andrew Charles Mynarski VC

clothing and saluted, before he jumped out of the aircraft. Pilot Officer Mynarski's descent was seen by French people on the ground. Both his parachute and clothing were on fire. He was found eventually by the French, but was so severely burnt that he died from his injuries.

The rear gunner had a miraculous escape when the aircraft crashed. He subsequently testified that, had Pilot Officer Mynarski not attempted to save his comrade's life, he could have left the aircraft in safety and would, doubtless, have escaped death.

Pilot Officer Mynarski must have been fully aware that in trying to free the rear gunner he was almost certain to lose his own life. Despite this, with outstanding courage and complete disregard for his own safety, he went to the rescue. Willingly accepting the danger, Pilot Officer Mynarski lost his life by a most conspicuous act of heroism which called for valour of the highest order.

Personal note: Pilot Officer Mynarski was born in Winnipeg and joined the Royal Canadian Air Force in 1941 as a wireless operator/air gunner. He was posted to England in 1943 and was commissioned in 1944. He was 28 years old.

Acting Wing Commander Guy Penrose Gibson VC, DSO, DFC

Acting Wing Commander Guy Penrose Gibson, DSO, DFC (39438), Reserve of Air Force Officers, No 617 Squadron.

This officer served as a night bomber pilot at the beginning of the war and quickly established a reputation as an outstanding operational pilot. In addition to taking the fullest possible share in all normal operations, he made single-handed attacks during his 'rest' nights on such highly defended objectives as the German battleship 'Tirpitz', then completing in Wilhelmshaven.

When his tour of operational duty was completed, he asked for a further operational posting and went to a night fighter unit instead of being posted for instructional duties. In the course of his second operational tour, he destroyed at least three enemy bombers and contributed much to the raising and development of new night fighter formations.

After a short period in a training unit, he again volunteered for operational duties and returned to night bombers. Both as an operational pilot and as leader of his squadron, he achieved outstandingly successful results and his personal courage knew no bounds. Berlin, Cologne, Danzig, Gdynia, Genoa, Le Creusot, Milan, Nuremberg and Stuttgart were among the targets he attacked by day and by night.

On the conclusion of his third operational tour, Wing Commander Gibson pressed strongly to be allowed to remain on operations and he was selected to command a squadron then forming for special tasks. Under his inspiring leadership, this squadron has now executed one of the most devastating attacks of the war – the breaching of the Moehne and Eder dams.

The task was fraught with danger and difficulty. Wing Commander Gibson personally made the initial attack on the Moehne dam. Descending to within a few feet of the water and taking the full brunt of the anti-aircraft defences, he delivered his attack with great accuracy. Afterwards, he circled very low for 30 minutes drawing the enemy fire on himself in order to leave as free a run as possible to the following aircraft which were attacking the dam in turn.

Wing Commander Gibson then led the remainder of his force to the Eder dam where, with complete disregard for his own safety, he repeated his tactics and once more drew on himself the enemy fire so that the attack could be successfully developed.

Wing Commander Gibson has completed over 170 sorties, involving more than 600 hours' operational flying. Throughout his operational career, prolonged exceptionally at his own request, he has shown leadership, determination and valour of the highest order.

Notes on career: Wing Commander Gibson was born at Simla in India in 1918. He was educated at St George's School, Folkestone and St Edward's School, Oxford. Commissioned in 1937, he won the DFC in July 1940, the Bar to DFC in September 1941, DSO in November 1942, Bar to DSO in March 1943. He was killed on 19th September

1944 when flying in a Mosquito as the Master Bomber on a raid against Rheydt. He crashed in Holland on the return journey.

Acting Squadron Leader Robert Anthony Maurice Palmer, DFC (115772), Royal Air Force Volunteer Reserve, No 109 Squadron, (Missing).

This officer has completed 110 bombing missions. Most of them involved deep penetration of heavily defended territory; many were low-level 'marking' operations against vital targets; all were executed with tenacity, high courage and great accuracy.

He first went on operations in January 1941. He took part in the first 1,000-bomber raid against Cologne in 1942. He was one of the first pilots to drop a 4,000-lb bomb on the Reich. It was known that he could be relied on to press home his attack whatever the opposition and to bomb with great accuracy. He was always selected, therefore, to take part in special operations against vital targets.

The finest example of his courage and determination was on 23rd December 1944 when he led a formation of Lancasters to attack the marshalling yards at Cologne in daylight. He had the task of marking the target and his formation had been ordered to bomb as soon as the bombs had gone from his, the leading aircraft.

The leader's duties during the final bombing run were exacting and demanded coolness and resolution. To achieve accuracy he would have to fly at an exact height and air speed on a steady course, regardless of opposition.

Some minutes before the target was reached, his aircraft came under heavy anti-aircraft fire, shells burst all around, two engines were set on fire and there were flames and smoke in the nose and in the bomb bay.

Enemy fighters now attacked in force. Squadron Leader Palmer disdained the possibility of taking avoiding action. He knew that if he diverged the least bit from his course, he would

Acting Squadron Leader Robert Anthony Maurice Palmer VC, DFC

be unable to utilise the special equipment to the best advantage. He was determined to complete the run and provide an accurate and easily seen aiming point for the other bombers. He ignored the double risk of fire and explosion in his aircraft and kept on. With its engines developing unequal power, an immense effort was needed to keep the damaged aircraft on a straight course. Nevertheless, he made a perfect approach and his bombs hit the target.

His aircraft was last seen spiralling to earth in flames. Such was the strength of the opposition that more than half of his formation failed to return.

Squadron Leader Palmer was an outstanding pilot. He displayed conspicuous bravery. His record of prolonged and heroic endeavour is beyond praise.

Personal note: Squadron Leader Palmer was only 24 when he won his Victoria Cross. He had been promoted Squadron Leader at 23 and altogether flew 110 operational missions. He already held the Distinguished Flying Cross and Bar.

Captain Edwin Swales VC, DFC

Captain Edwin Swales, DFC (6101V), South African Air Force, No 582 Squadron, (Deceased).

Captain Swales was 'master bomber' of a force of aircraft which attacked Pforzheim on the night of 23rd February 1945. As 'master bomber', he had the task of locating the target area with precision and of giving aiming instructions to the main force of bombers following in his wake.

Soon after he had reached the target area he was engaged by an enemy fighter and one of his engines was put out of action. His rear guns failed. His crippled aircraft was an easy prey to further attacks. Unperturbed, he carried on with his allotted task; clearly and precisely he issued aiming instructions to the main force. Meanwhile the enemy fighter closed the range and fired again. A second engine of Captain Swales' aircraft was put out of action. Almost defenceless, he stayed over the target area issuing his aiming instructions until he was satisfied that the attack had achieved its purpose.

It is now known that the attack was one of the most concentrated and successful of the war.

Captain Swales did not, however, regard his mission as completed. His aircraft was damaged. Its speed had been so much reduced that it could only with difficulty be kept in the air. The blind-flying instruments were no longer working. Determined at all costs to prevent his aircraft and crew from falling into enemy hands, he set course for home. After an hour he flew into thin-layered cloud. He kept his course by skilful flying between the layers, but later heavy cloud and turbulent air conditions were met. The aircraft, by now over friendly territory, became more and more difficult to control; it was losing height steadily. Realising that the situation was desperate Captain Swales ordered his crew to bale out. Time was very short and it required all his exertions to keep the aircraft steady while each of his crew moved in turn to the escape hatch and parachuted to safety. Hardly had the last crew-member jumped when the aircraft plunged to earth. Captain Swales was found dead at the controls.

Intrepid in the attack, courageous in the face of danger, he did his duty to the last, giving his life that his comrades might live.

Personal notes: Captain Swales was a South African born in Durban. He served first in the Army and was with the Eighth Army throughout the North African campaign. He transferred to the South African Air Force in June 1943 and trained as a pilot. He was posted to England and flew with the Pathfinder Force until his death, at the age of 29, in the last months of the war.

905192 Sergeant (now Warrant Officer) Norman Cyril Jackson, RAFVR, No 106 Squadron.

This airman was the flight engineer in a Lancaster detailed to attack Schweinfurt on the night of 26th April 1944. Bombs were dropped successfully and the aircraft was climbing out of the target area. Suddenly it was attacked by a fighter at about 20,000 feet. The captain took evading action at once, but the enemy secured many hits. A fire started near a petrol tank on the upper surface of the starboard wing, between the fuselage and the inner engine.

Sergeant Jackson was thrown to the floor during the engagement. Wounds which he received from shell splinters in the right leg and shoulder were probably sustained at that time. Recovering himself he remarked that he could deal with the fire on the wing and obtained his captain's permission to try to put out the flames.

Pushing a hand fire-extinguisher into the top of his life-saving jacket and clipping on his parachute pack, Sergeant Jackson jettisoned the escape hatch above the pilot's head. He then started to climb out of the cockpit and back along the top of the fuselage to the starboard wing. Before he could leave the fuselage his parachute pack opened and the whole canopy and rigging lines spilled into the cockpit.

Undeterred, Sergeant Jackson continued. The pilot, bomb aimer and navigator gathered the parachute together and held on to the rigging lines, paying them out as the airman crawled aft. Eventually he slipped and, falling from the fuselage to the starboard wing, grasped an air intake on the leading edge of the wing. He succeeded in clinging on but lost the extinguisher, which was blown away.

By this time, the fire had spread rapidly and Sergeant Jackson was involved. His face, hands and clothing were severely burnt. Unable to retain his hold he was swept through the flames and over the trailing edge of the wing, dragging his parachute behind. When last seen it was only partly inflated and was burning in a number of places.

Realising that the fire could not be controlled, the captain gave the order to abandon aircraft. Four of the remaining members of the crew landed safely. The captain and rear gunner have not been accounted for.

Sergeant Jackson was unable to control his descent and landed heavily. He sustained a broken ankle, his right eye was closed through burns and his hands were useless. These injuries, together with the wounds received

Warrant Officer Norman Cyril Jackson VC

earlier, reduced him to a pitiable state. At daybreak he crawled to the nearest village where he was taken prisoner. He bore the intense pain and discomfort of the journey to Dulag Luft with magnificent fortitude. After 10 months in hospital he made a good recovery, though his hands require further treatment and are only of limited use.

The airman's attempt to extinguish the fire and save the aircraft and crew from falling into enemy hands was an act of outstanding gallantry. To venture outside, when travelling at 200 miles an hour, at a great height and in intense cold, was an almost incredible feat. Had he succeeded in subduing the flames, there was little or no prospect of his regaining the cockpit. The spilling of his parachute and the risk of grave damage to its canopy reduced his chances of survival to a minimum. By his ready willingness to face these dangers he set an example of self-sacrifice which will ever be remembered.

Personal note: Warrant Officer Jackson was born in 1919 at Ealing. He was a fitter in civilian life and joined the Royal Air Force in October 1939. His first operational tour was with Coastal Command and he joined Bomber Command in 1943. He had completed 30 operations with No. 106 Squadron up to the time of his capture.

Flight Sergeant George Thompson VC

1370700 Flight Sergeant George Thompson. Royal Air Force Volunteer Reserve, No 9 Squadron Bomber Command (Deceased).

This airman was the wireless operator in a Lancaster aircraft which attacked the Dortmund-Ems Canal in daylight on the 1st January 1945.

The bombs had just been released when a heavy shell hit the aircraft in front of the mid-upper turret. Fire broke out and dense smoke filled the fuselage. The nose of the aircraft was then hit and an inrush of air, clearing the smoke, revealed a scene of utter devastation. Most of the perspex screen of the nose compartment had been shot away, gaping holes has been torn in the canopy above the pilot's head, the inter-communication wiring was severed, and there was a large hole in the floor of the aircraft. Bedding and other equipment were badly damaged or alight; one engine was on fire.

Flight Sergeant Thompson saw that the gunner was unconscious in the blazing mid-upper turret. Without hesitation he went down the fuselage into the fire and the exploding ammunition. He pulled the gunner from his turret and, edging his way round the hole in the floor, carried him away from the flames. With his bare hands, he extinguished the gunner's burning clothing. He himself sustained serious burns on his face, hands and legs.

Flight Sergeant Thompson then noticed that the rear gun turret was also on fire. Despite his own severe injuries he moved painfully to the rear of the fuselage where he found the rear gunner with his clothing alight, overcome by flames and fumes. A second time Flight Sergeant Thompson braved the flames. With great difficulty he extricated the helpless gunner and carried him clear. Again, he used his bare hands, already burnt, to beat out flames on a comrade's clothing.

Flight Sergeant Thompson, by now almost exhausted, felt that his duty was not yet done. He must report the fate of the crew to the captain. He made the perilous journey back through the burning fuselage, clinging to the sides with his burnt hands to get across the hole in the floor. The flow of cold air caused him intense pain and frost-bite developed. So pitiful was his condition that his captain failed to recognise him. Still, his only concern was for the two gunners he had left in the rear of the aircraft. He was given such attention as was possible until a crash landing was made some forty minutes later.

When the aircraft was hit, Flight Sergeant Thompson might have devoted his efforts to quelling the fire and so have contributed to his own safety. He preferred to go through the fire to succour his comrades. He knew that he would then be in no position to hear or heed any order which might be given to abandon aircraft. He hazarded his own life in order to save the lives of others. Young in years and experience, his actions were those of a veteran.

Three weeks later Flight Sergeant Thompson died of his injuries. One of the gunners unfortunately also died, but the other owes his life to the superb gallantry of Flight Sergeant Thompson, whose signal courage and self-sacrifice will ever be an inspiration to the Service.

Personal note: George Thompson, a former grocer's assistant, won his Victoria Cross at the age of 24. He was a Scot and he joined the Air Force in 1941. He did not become an air wireless operator until 1944 and had only been on operations for two months before his death.

Acting Squadron Leader Ian Willoughby Bazalgette, DFC (118131), Royal Air Force Volunteer Reserve, No 635 Squadron, (Deceased).

On 4th August 1944, Squadron Leader Bazalgette was 'master bomber' of a Pathfinder Squadron detailed to mark an important target at Trossy St Maximin for the main bomber force.

When nearing the target his Lancaster came under heavy anti-aircraft fire. Both starboard engines were put out of action and serious fires broke out in the fuselage and the starboard mainplane. The bomb aimer was badly wounded.

As the deputy 'master bomber' had already been shot down, the success of the attack depended on Squadron Leader Bazalgette and this he knew. Despite the appalling conditions in his burning aircraft, he pressed on gallantly to the target, marking and bombing it accurately. That the attack was successful was due to his magnificent effort.

After the bombs had been dropped the Lancaster dived, practically out of control. By expert airmanship and great exertion Squadron Leader Bazalgette regained control. But the port inner engine then failed and the whole of the starboard mainplane became a mass of flames.

Squadron Leader Bazalgette fought bravely to bring his aircraft and crew to safety. The mid-upper gunner was overcome by fumes. Squadron Leader Bazalgette then ordered those of his

Acting Squadron Leader Ian Willoughby Bazalgette VC, DFC

crew who were able to leave by parachute to do so. He remained at the controls and attempted the almost hopeless task of landing the crippled and blazing aircraft in a last effort to save the wounded bomb aimer and helpless air gunner. With superb skill, and taking great care to avoid a small French village nearby, he brought the aircraft down safely. Unfortunately, it then exploded and this gallant officer and his two comrades perished.

His heroic sacrifice marked the climax of a long career of operations against the enemy. He always chose the more dangerous and exacting roles. His courage and devotion to duty were beyond praise.

Personal notes: Squadron Leader Bazalgette was 26 years old. Born in Calgary, Alberta, he was brought up in England and joined the army in 1940. He transferred to the Royal Air Force in 1941 and was on his second tour of operations when he won his Victoria Cross. He had already been awarded the Distinguished Flying Cross in his first for bravery in a low level attack on Milan in July 1943.